Early Praise for
Serendipitously Rich

"What if it really is simpler than you ever thought, easier than you ever imagined, and more fun than you ever dared dream – to get rich (or anything else you want)? Madeleine Kay shows you that this is not only true . . . but that it is *so* simple, you will kick yourself for not thinking of it before!"

> – Randy Gilbert, President and CEO
> Inside Success Productions, LLC

"A Great Read! Madeleine Kay's *Serendipitously Rich* provides a very simple, extremely empowering yet seemingly effortless process for getting out of your head, into your heart, and unleashing the magic within you to get whatever you want."

> – Chuck Danes, www.Abundance-and-Happiness.com

"The subtitle of this book should be *'There won't be any more excuses for not getting rich (or anything else you want)!'* If you are ready to get rich and influence the world to get what you want . . . then read this book."

> – Jon Berghoff, President, Global Empowerment
> Connection, www.geconnection.com

"*Serendipitously Rich* is excitingly original and refreshingly new! And what a lively and joyful read it is. It will not only help you . . . it will actually help you to get the riches you desire."

> – Rick Frishman, ~~~~~~~~~~~~~~~~~~~~~~~~~~~~
> including *Where's* ~~~~~~~~~~

"Madeleine Kay brilliantly teaches ~~~~~~~~~~~~~~
need to do to change *if* I were rich t~~~~~
to eliminate money as an obstacle t~~~~~

> – Marcia Wieder, Founder & CEO, Dream University

"In Madeleine Kay's latest book *Serendipitously Rich*, I was immediately sucked into her psychology on how she effortlessly uses the law of attraction, in such a practical way, to create true wealth. This is a must read for anyone who wants to become rich FAST."

– Dr. Richard M. Krawczyk, Bestselling Author of *Financial Aerobics: How to Get Your Finances into Shape*, www.RichardLIVE.com

"*Serendipitously Rich* is original, it's simple, it's fun to read . . . and her message works! Though the topic is significant and real, Madeleine's approach is light and lively – a real 'pick-me-up.' It's a fresh, upbeat look at important and timeless principles."

– Leslie Householder, Author of *The Jackrabbit Factor*

"This book really delivers! *Serendipitously Rich* takes the need for complicating, angsting, worrying, planning, strategizing, struggling and trying, out of a subject that has been over-complicated, over-strategized and over-technologized. Madeleine Kay shows you how to *just* do it – easily, simply, practically – and actually have fun doing it."

– Karen Williams, Idealistic Baby Boomer who has discovered she has not planned for retirement

"This is the best book I have ever read on the subject of success, making money and getting what you want – and I have read them all! If you read only one book on the subject – make it this one."

– Lainie Collins, President, Purely Sensational Enterprises

"This book gave me permission to do what I want . . . AND make lots of money! It turned my fear into excitement, my hesitations to proaction, my worry to anticipation, and my anxiety to exhilaration. This book works. It's not theory. It's not abstract mumbo-jumbo. It's not a business plan. Anyone can do this! It's such practical, usable 'real-life' stuff."

– Carol Smith, Former Homeless Person

"*Serendipitously Rich* was truly a delight to read. Being fairly picky about how the Law of Attraction is taught, I smiled more as I turned every page, thoroughly engaged with the writing style, and the content! All the important elements of a good Law of Attraction education were there, and some that aren't talked about NEARLY enough in other books. One of my new favorites for sure!"

"If you want to activate your 'on' switch, your 'go' switch, your whatever it is that makes you 'do' something switch . . . read *Serendipitously Rich!*"

"In *Serendipitously Rich*, Madeleine Kay offers insights to help you experience riches in all areas of your life. It is my hope that *Serendipitously Rich* brings you all the riches you desire!"

"In *Serendipitously Rich*, Madeleine Kay poses a Dare and a Double Dare that are deliciously compelling! I dare you to read this book and not absolutely love it! I double dare you to read it and not get all the riches you desire!"

. . . .

For all of you
who want something more practical and concrete
than general, abstract metaphysical theory . . .

For everyone who
craves something simpler, easier, more fun and less
overwhelming than complicated strategies, business
plans and technical programs . . .

***Serendipitously Rich* shows you**
how to stop struggling and how to start getting rich
(and everything else you want) . . . and begin savoring your life.

SERENDIPITOUSLY RICH

MADELEINE KAY

SERENDIPITOUSLY
RICH

How to Get Delightfully,
Delectably, Deliciously Rich
(or anything else you want)
in 7 Ridiculously Easy Steps

New York

Serendipitously Rich by Madeleine Kay
www.SerendipitouslyRich.com

Paperback ISBN: 978-1-60037-493-7
Hardback ISBN: 978-1-60037-494-4
Library of Congress: 2008934124
First Edition

Published by:

MORGAN · JAMES
THE ENTREPRENEURIAL PUBLISHER™
www.morganjamespublishing.com

Morgan James Publishing, LLC
1225 Franklin Ave. Ste. 325
Garden City, NY 11530-1693
Toll Free 800-485-4943
www.MorganJamesPublishing.com

Cover Design by Ben Clark
ben@bigbenmedia.com

Interior Design by Debra A. Perkins
perkygraphics@charter.net
and Claire Collins

DEDICATION

To my father
Harry Tckaz Kay

. . . .

fOREWORD

Madeleine Kay is the greatest motivator I know! She makes things so simple, so easy, and so natural, that you just do them. You don't think, you don't plan, you don't wonder "how." You just do it!

And by just doing it, you transport yourself into a whole other dimension – one that is energized by a momentum, an enthusiasm, a passion and a belief that make you unstoppable, so success is assured and your dreams already a reality.

In *Serendipitously Rich*, she gets you to act not think. She gets you to do, not plan. She sets you in motion by igniting something inside you that has probably been longing to be fueled for a long time, but couldn't find the spark . . . Madeleine is that spark.

Reading *Serendipitously Rich* will thoroughly transform your life . . . making it richer and more abundant in every way. It is so amazingly simple, practical, down-to-earth and immediately do-able, that you will not believe you never thought of it before . . . and you will be glad you know it now, so you can just *do* it – whatever *It* is to you.

I'm the guy in the movie *The Secret* who stressed the Universe likes speed. You have to take action to get anything done. But that action doesn't have to be work. It can be easy, effortless and fun – and that's what Madeleine shows you how to do.

Why do I like this book? Because it *is* so easy, effortless and fun. And . . . it works! Turn the page and let the magic begin!

– Joe Vitale, Bestselling Author of *The Attractor Factor:*
5 Easy Steps for Creating Wealth (or Anything Else) From the
Inside Out and Featured Star in *The Secret*, www.mrfire.com

CONTENTS

. . . .

Chapter 9

OTHER BOOKS
BY MADELEINE KAY

Non-Fiction

Living Serendipitously . . . keeping the wonder alive
(www.livingserendipitously.com)

Living with Outrageous Joy
(www.livingwithoutrageousjoy.com)

E-Books

~~Filthy Obscenely~~ Deliciously Rich and Loving It . . .
How to Get Rich (or anything else you want)
in 6 Really Easy Steps
(www.deliciouslyrich.com)

The UMM Factor . . .
(what you need in order to succeed)
(www.ummfactor.com)

Acknowledgments

To my mother, Anne Kay, for *everything*;

To my son, Daniel Sage (Bar-Sadeh), for just being and who, in so many ways, paves the way for me;

To my wonderful friends – especially Manuela Cobos, Yves Debarge, Ellen Latimer, Janie Lotierzo, Hope Marcus, Lisabeth Reynolds, Federico Velludo and Claude Zeligman – for their continuous love and support that mean so much to me and always give me that shot of adrenalin whenever I need it;

To my friends, Haze Wainberg and Renzo and Delores Favaretto, whose shining examples have inspired and guided me;

To everyone who has ever inspired and motivated me;

To the entire team at Morgan James Publishing, especially Jim Howard and Margo Toulouse, for their guidance and support;

To my very good friend, mentor and motivator, Don Green at the Napoleon Hill Foundation, who has believed in and supported me with his unbounded enthusiasm from the moment we met;

To Randy Gilbert, at Inside Success Productions, for being a visionary and seeing the possibilities;

To my dog Yoda, for finding me;

To Debbie Perkins, for helping me get everything together;

To my graphic designer – my *everything* person, Claire Collins, without whom none of this would have ever been possible;

And to God, Love and Life . . . to *this moment* . . . so rich and ripe with possibilities . . . *thank you.*

A Note from the Author

I was astounded to discover how easy it is to become rich . . . how easy it is to acquire real wealth with relative ease and to do, be and have everything you want, once I applied the principles by which I have lived my life to the art of making money.

As an artist who has always been motivated by spiritual and aesthetic values, I was never interested before in making money, never even thought of living serendipitously as it applies to becoming wealthy. It just wasn't part of my vocabulary . . . nor anything I was particularly inspired by.

Now I realize that I was arbitrarily limiting myself and living serendipitously to only certain aspects of life, which I believed were worthy and noble. I now know that living serendipitously applies to ALL of life – even money – and that making money, lots of it, is worthy and noble. That money is good . . . and being wealthy is spiritual. That you can be a good, kind, generous, compassionate person and still have gads of money and be staggeringly wealthy.

Although I speak specifically about acquiring money and becoming wealthy in this book, the steps in this book can be applied to anything you want in life since the ultimate goal of life is to live all of life as richly and fully as we can. And money (or the lack of it) is too often the excuse people use for not living richly. So I want to share with you the secrets I have discovered – the 7 ridiculously easy, sure-fire steps for acquiring money, becoming wealthy, and for getting anything . . . no . . . *everything* you want in life.

Madeleine Kay

SERENDIPITOUSLY
RICH

INTRODUCTION

*H*ave you ever noticed the words we use when referring to money? "He's filthy rich!" or "She's obscenely wealthy." We refer to money as "dirty" and people who care about or want or have money as greedy and selfish.

No wonder so many people don't have money and live in lack . . . and then wonder why! They don't *want* money. They don't want to be filthy, obscene, greedy or selfish . . . so on a very strong subliminal level, probably most of you who do not now have money or are not wealthy, are in your present situation because you don't and haven't ever really wanted money.

I know you probably find that hard to believe and are even sitting there saying, "Of course I want money! Who doesn't?"

You don't. And I didn't either for a long time. Oh sure, you say you want money, you want to get out of debt. But the part of you that attracts whatever you experience in your life, the part of you that really on a core, elemental level is determining what you really want and therefore, will get, have and experience, has disdain for money, little or no respect for money, and doesn't even like money.

I realized this a while ago when I was having financial difficulties and was in fact, in major debt. Although I said I wanted money, I wanted to be rich, I wanted to get out of debt . . . on a deep core level, I did NOT want money because I thought it would change who I was. I thought it would diminish me in some way.

THE ISSUE WITH MONEY

Let me back track a little to explain, because so many of us have issues with money that are so subtle and totally unknown to our conscious minds that we aren't even aware of them. Our relationship with money is very complex and often confusing. So let me explain a few things . . . and see if any of these apply to you. See if they resonate with you . . . Be honest with yourself because if you ever want to be rich . . . really rich

. . . you have to recognize, acknowledge and then discard and replace your old beliefs about money and wealth with new, healthy, productive beliefs, which is really hard to do if you're not even aware of your beliefs to begin with.

It's easy to do once you become conscious of your beliefs. Then you just replace those beliefs with new, healthier, more productive ones. If you are reading this book, then you are ready for a change . . . like getting rid of old clothes that no longer fit you or you no longer feel good in, and replacing them with new ones that make you feel and look like a million bucks!

Wouldn't it be great to put on something every day that you feel just sensational in? Well, that's how your whole life can and should be – every single day can be like a favorite outfit that you love. Every day can and should be special. And . . . you can do, be and have everything you want . . . right now, without sacrificing your soul to get it.

I guess that's the key phrase – "without sacrificing your soul to get it" – whatever *it* is. So many of us have been preprogrammed to believe that to become wealthy or be successful, we need to "sell our soul." That we will be forced to compromise our integrity and values and somehow diminish who we are . . . put our very authenticity into question.

That's how I felt for most of my life. I was an artist . . . a writer, and felt therefore, that I should not care about money or success. They were beneath me. In fact, I think that if I had written a book years ago and someone or some company had offered me a $500,000 advance or royalty, I would have actually turned it down. I probably would have stuck up my nose and said quite sincerely, "Oh no, I'm an artist. I don't care about money," and walked away.

Now I know that sounds ridiculous to you . . . and to me too now because I am making it so obvious. But years ago, it wasn't so obvious to me. I was stuck in "the starving artist syndrome" – that to be a true artist, a great artist, you had to create for one reason only – the love of the art and creating – and you could not, should not, dare not want, care about or even be willing to accept money (especially a lot of money!) for it, because that would somehow taint your artistic integrity and the value of what you had created.

So yes, years ago, I would have walked away from millions . . . and probably did. As we all have. I sabotaged myself and my success so many times, often without even being aware of it . . . as I am sure so many of you have too.

I had no idea I was doing it though. I thought I was being noble and good and "true to myself." What hogwash! The truth is I had issues about money that I was not even aware of (more about those later). Perhaps I was also afraid of success – the responsibility, the work, the demands and expectations that come with success. Perhaps I was lazy. Perhaps I was just ignorant about a lot of things and needed to do a lot more living and learning before I was ready to be successful . . . ready to be rich . . . ready to make friends with money.

Anyway, one morning it hit me . . . that I didn't really *want* money. I had no respect for money. I didn't even like money. So why should money come to me, I realized. Why in the world would anything or anyone be attracted to or come to someone who doesn't want it, doesn't respect it and doesn't even like it?

Wow! I was stunned! It was an amazing epiphany for me that changed my life. I had mismanaged money – lots of it! I had squandered money, saying, "Oh, it's only money," (I'm sure you've heard that before!) dismissing it as though money was insignificant and had no value at all.

Now I am not saying that money is all-important either. What I am saying is that money, like so many other things in life, is important and can and should not be dismissed. It should not be sought only because we have to have money to live or survive. It should be sought not as an end in itself, but for its exchange value in terms of time, energy, relationships, goods and the service we can do . . . for the freedom it affords us to fully develop our potential and to use all our talents, without dissipating any of those because we are living in lack, anxiety, worry or fear, which drain all our resources, both spiritual and practical.

Money *does* indeed have value – positive value. I had gone to such an extreme in my disdain for money, riches and success, because I thought that disdain and disinterest in them confirmed the fact that I was a good person, an honest person, a sincere person whose values were lofty and noble that . . . Not only did my lack of interest in money not make me any of those things, it made me foolish and put me in debt . . . and seriously affected the quality of my life on every level.

And here's the interesting thing. When I had that epiphany and finally realized the intrinsic value of money – the freedom it affords one to truly live as one wants, to create, to share, to be generous, to be spiritual, to live openly and totally from the heart – I felt ashamed of myself. I felt like somehow I had become or admitted that I am a superficial person with no real values at all.

And when I spoke to my son about this book I wanted to write (to share this with as many people as possible so they/you too could become deliciously rich by liberating yourselves from your insidiously subtle limiting beliefs about money and your right to be rich), I couldn't bring myself to tell him what I really wanted to write about. I kept beating around the bush so I wouldn't have to admit that I wanted to be rich, that I cared about money, and that I actually wanted to write a book about it. I thought he would be disappointed in me.

I kept trying to make the book sound more like a spiritual book because I still couldn't reconcile myself to the fact that money IS spiritual . . . and that being rich is noble and that wealth is a desirable thing that enhances one's entire life – mind, body and spirit. It enables you to fully integrate the various parts of yourself and to truly "savor" your life in a manner that is so deliciously *wholistic* and holistic.

Kind of like years ago, when people (mostly women) couldn't admit that they liked sex – that they enjoyed it and wanted it. They thought it made them seem less wholesome and spiritual. Well, not only is sex rampant in the *Bible* and an integral part of all religions . . . it is the only way we procreate and create new life! Think of it . . . it is the very foundation of all of life . . . and the ultimate act of creation. So, why shouldn't we like sex?

Fortunately, as my son and I spoke, he kept asking me questions and probing (not about sex, but about what I wanted to write in this book) and finally, after forty-five minutes, he got me to the point where I admitted that I do like money and what it can do for me. And that yes, I wanted to write about it. It was, for me, a very healing conversation that brought me to a whole new level of understanding and acceptance. And quite to my surprise, I think it was very healing for my son too. He's also an artist – a musician – and my admission gave him permission to admit that he too wants to be rich and wants to be paid well for his efforts and creations.

I was even nervous about writing an e-mail about all this to the people on my website e-mail list, because it talked about money. I thought the people on my list would shun me, feel like I was a traitor of some sort . . . that they would all unsubscribe. But they didn't. Not a single person unsubscribed. Some of them even wrote back to thank me for writing the e-mail. (I have included a copy of the e-mail at the end of this introduction. It is titled *Money is Energy.*)

But my acceptance of the integration of money and spirituality still wasn't complete. I kept back-sliding. Every time I thought about writing this book (and others on the subjects of wealth, success and becoming rich . . . subjects about which I am now passionate), I shuddered, thinking that my friends and readers will think I have become shallow, that I have sold out, that I am no longer a spiritual person with lofty values.

But like Nietzsche says in the prologue to his book *Thus Spake Zarathustra*, I have become "like the bee that hath gathered too much honey; I need hands outstretched to take it." I am so excited about this realization that has absolutely liberated me, that has completely opened up my entire life to all of life . . . to *everything* it has to offer . . . that I can't wait to share it with you. I can't wait to tell you how easy it is to transform your life and become truly rich and prosperous.

So yes, I now know that living a rich and abundant life is both noble and desirable; that you can do more good and help more people if you are wealthy rather than poor; that feeling bad about surpassing your parents is not a way of honoring them, but of dishonoring them; that artistic creation has real value and deserves to be compensated just like any other job or profession; that I and all of us are truly meant to be rich and to do, be and have it all; and that money and spirit are both the same . . . they are all energy – the currency of our lives.

I know that our lives, in order to be vibrant, full of vitality, succulent and ripe with possibilities, are waiting for us to claim them in all their splendor, variety and richness. In claiming my riches, I have reclaimed my life . . . and I invite you to do the same.

MONEY iS ENERGY

I have heard that said over and over in the last ten years.

Both physics and metaphysics tell us the same thing . . . that everything is energy. There is a universal energy of which we are all a part and which is the source and substance of everything, including us.

I get it. I understand it. Well, I sort of understand it in terms of its exchange value and quotient. But I never really got it until about two years ago.

I was visiting a good friend of mine in Canada. She is staggeringly wealthy . . . and has been ever since she was born.

She has always had an unbelievably high energy level, a stamina that leaves everyone else in the dust, and a quality of vitality that never loses its radiant glow and momentum.

This everyone knows about her and just accepts. Like the perennial EverReady battery, she seems unstoppable . . . she just keeps going and going and going with an enthusiasm and a level of performance that never wane.

Well, two years ago, while I was visiting her and trying dismally and unsuccessfully to keep up with her, it hit me! I suddenly knew why and how she is the way she is . . . Money!

Yes – money! Do you realize how much energy people put into thinking about money, making money, planning for money, worrying about money, scrounging for money, shifting things around to get more money?? And the list goes on and on . . . It's exhausting!

Now imagine a lifetime of doing that! Do you realize the amount of energy a person uses up in his or her lifetime over money concerns?

Now . . . imagine a lifetime of NEVER doing that? That's right! Can you imagine the energy reserve my friend has that 99.99% of everyone else does not have?

No wonder she has so much more energy than everyone else! She has never, ever had to use or expend a drop of her energy thinking about money, worrying about it, planning for it, doing things to get it – so the "balance" in her energy bank account is filled to the brim and constantly overflowing with unused energy that everyone else has expended.

So, I finally got it! It was no longer a mere abstraction for me when I would read that "money is energy." I even realized that the saying "spend your energy," is talking about just that . . . that both money and energy are the currency of our lives. It has given me a new, healthy respect for and appreciation of money (both of which I never had before) as something that is not separate from my spiritual self, but rather, an integral part of the "whole" of me . . . something that actually contributes to my happiness, my evolution as a human being and my overall well-being.

Integrating this reality into my life as a spiritual person motivated by aesthetic values and beauty has been an exciting and liberating challenge. It has opened up the entire world for me . . . and made all things possible . . . and yes, even desirable.

. . . .

So . . . LIVE SERENDIPITOUSLY . . .
ENJOY . . . PROSPER . . .
AND DARE TO BE RICH!

Madeleine
"The Serendipity Lady"

1

THE 12 MYTHS ABOUT MONEY

Before we jump into the first step in becoming rich, let's quickly dispense with some of the limiting beliefs and erroneous myths so many of us have about money, becoming rich and being wealthy, so we can get them out of the way and move on to the real business of becoming rich.

(I am not even going to capitalize, bold or highlight these myths, or even make them stand-alone sentences or paragraphs, because I do not want them to stand out on the page and there-fore, in your minds.)

Myth #1

*I*t is noble to be poor or at least not too rich. This is a wide-spread myth that is truly insidious and I believe has caused no end of damage to allowing people to believe that they have a right to be rich.

You do not in any way help or honor those who are living in lack by also living in lack. The only way you can help them is by being a shining example of how well they too can live and by teaching them and/or giving them the tools they need to elevate their own standard of living.

Lowering your standard of living or keeping your standards low so you don't hurt, offend or frustrate those who are living at a low standard, not only doesn't help them; it further cements them in their own rut and gives them a convenient excuse not to rise above it.

Myth #2

*I*f I have a lot of money or more than I need, then I am taking something away from others who could use it more. This myth is based on a belief in lack and limitation and a finite universe.

There is an infinite supply of abundant wealth, health and happiness for every other person in this world. Your having a lot, even to excess, does not in any way diminish the chances or opportunities for anyone else to have whatever he or she wants, nor does it take anything away from anyone else.

In fact, it does just the opposite. Your abundance creates *an energy of abundance*, which it sends out into the universe . . . and since both physics and metaphysics tell us that everything is energy, your abundant energy just helps multiply the abundance that is available and accessible to everyone else.

Myth #3

I should feel guilty about surpassing or living better than my parents. This is a very subtle myth that most people aren't even aware of, and it doesn't even necessarily come from anything your parents may have done or said. In fact, I find it often is totally self-imposed, for a variety of reasons (which I am not even going to get into here because it is too much of a digression and not really relevant).

Not only does not living better than your parents not honor them, it is a way of dishonoring them and all the sacrifices they have made for you. The best way to honor your parents and your ancestors, to celebrate their lives and show appreciation for their sacrifices, is to live as happily and as well and as richly as you possibly can.

In fact, it is the hope and prayer of every parent that their children will have better, easier lives than they have. That is the very reason your parents made those sacrifice in the first place.

Myth #4

Rich people are not very nice and are very superficial. That attitude is to me, a supreme act of arrogance and quite prejudicial.

Rich people are just like people who are not rich – some are nice, some are not; some are superficial, some are not. It is not the money that makes the person, it is the person's values and character that make him or her who they are.

I think sometimes confidence is mistaken for arrogance, and people who have money tend to have a lot more confidence than those who don't. It is true that many people who do not have much money are often more deferring than those with money. But do not mistake low self-esteem (which many people who do not have much money experience) for humility and character. And do not judge confidence as arrogance and superficiality.

I find also that many rich people are judged by those with less money because of envy or jealousy. Do not envy anyone . . . There is enough money and riches for everyone. Their having a lot does not take anything away from you and does not cast any aspersions on you, your abilities or your value or self-worth. Only you determine your value and self-worth. Only you determine how much of anything, including money, you will have.

Myth #5

If I am rich or care about making a lot of money, I will be less spiritual and will wind up compromising my values and integrity. This myth is steeped in a strong judgmental attitude and arises from a lack of understanding of how the universe really works.

Money is just as spiritual as work, religion, family, nature, sex . . . It's all part of life and none of it is "bad." It's all good, especially if everything is kept in balance and perspective, if we don't idolize or obsess about any one thing, if we strive to enjoy it all.

In the universe, there is one substance (some people call it One Mind) of which we are all a part . . . and this one substance is limitless and abundant. Money is part of that abundance and is therefore good and spiritual, because it is part of the All that is.

Again, I think there is a lot of envy and jealousy associated with this judgment. Since a lot of people don't have the money they would like to have and feel badly about it, they often – either as defense mechanism or to redirect their own frustration, anger or disappointment with themselves – transfer these emotions onto the wealthy and label them undesirable in some way . . . and in that way, make themselves feel better about not being one of the wealthy.

Myth #6

*I*f I care about money, it means that I am materialistic. This is one I wrestled with a lot when I was growing up . . . and well into my adult years, especially when I was in a long-term relationship with a man who was the ultimate consumer.

It seems to me that if you truly use and enjoy the things you buy, then that doesn't make you materialistic. If those things enrich your life, then I don't think that makes you materialistic. I believe that materialism is only when a person feels he must have a lot of things, must accumulate a lot to make himself or herself feel worthy or accomplished, without any regard for the pleasure, joy and genuine enrichment one experiences from having and using those things.

I think we slap labels on people (ourselves included) and their actions far too quickly and easily without really taking the time to think about or understand the implications, value and intentions of their actions and behaviors.

Myth #7

*W*anting to make a lot of money or be rich is not a very worthwhile goal in life. Why not? I am discovering how much fun and exciting it is to make money. Everybody likes money, wants money, needs it and enjoys it . . . so why wouldn't it be worthwhile?

I remember about ten years ago, I was at my cousin's daughter's wedding and saw my cousin's ex-husband for the first time in years. I heard that he had recently gotten married after a long period of being single. So when I saw him, I said, "Hi, Carey. Congratulations. I am so glad to hear you are so happy;" to which he replied, "I don't know how happy I am, and besides, I'm not so sure happiness is such a worthwhile goal in life."

Wow! That says it all, doesn't it? He is highly educated and quite the intellectual, but I don't think he knows a whole lot about life and living because he is stuck in the arrogance that doesn't let him admit even the most elemental things about himself and his life because he is too proud and attached to his own image of himself.

Happiness is THE goal in life – it's what everyone wants . . . every single one of us. It is the reason we do *everything* in our lives . . . because we think it will make us happy. So why are so many of us reluctant, even ashamed to admit . . . perhaps even unaware of the fact that what we really want in life is just to be happy. Why does that seem too shallow or superficial to admit, accept or believe?

Why are so many of us reluctant and even ashamed to admit that we would like to be rich? Why does that make us feel as though we are shallow or superficial, and somehow, less noble . . . as if wanting to be rich precludes and excludes our wanting to do or be anything else as well?

Myth #8

You need to work very hard (and perhaps even "sell your soul") to make money and get rich. This idea comes from the fact that years ago, life was harder, and perhaps people did have to work harder to make money. I don't know if that was true years ago, or just seemed true from the many images we have of the masses during wars and the Depression, of people who may have been culturally and socially hypnotized and programmed with that ethos.

I do know that it is no longer true. You don't have to work hard to make money; you just have to work smart. They are very different. The old fashioned work ethic was, I believe, taken to such an extreme and inculcated in so many people, that many people feel really guilty if they don't work hard, if things come to them too easily. And that's when they begin to subconsciously sabotage themselves – to create problems, to cause difficulties so they will have to struggle and feel that they are "working for and really earning" whatever they get.

Myth #9

If things are too easy or good for me, God will think I

am arrogant and punish me or test me. This idea is closely aligned with a feeling that God is a punitive, judgmental God and that we do not live in a friendly universe.

Some religious concepts do promulgate the vision of a punitive God who judges, but for the most part, great minds through the ages and across all cultures have said the same thing – that we *do* live in a friendly universe that is benevolent. That we are part of the One Substance from which all things come and of which all life is made, and that One Substance is always loving, always for us. Each of us is like a hologram in which the whole is contained in the part. So while each of us is a piece of God, each of us is also All of God.

It seems to me that we create God in our own image, and it is we, not God therefore, who is punitive and judgmental. If we would cut ourselves and others a little slack and realize that we are not perfect, that we are a work in progress and that each of us is always doing the best we can at any given time, then perhaps we would no longer judge ourselves and others and project an image of a God who is judgmental and punitive. Instead, we will realize that God, the Universe, the Force, the One Mind – whatever you want to call the organizing principle of the universe – wants only *one* thing . . . our happiness, our well-being, our success . . . And then perhaps, we will feel comfortable with success and riches that come to us with ease.

Einstein said, "The single most important decision any of us will ever have to make is whether or not to believe that the universe is a friendly place."

Myth #10

*I*f I want a lot of money or I want to be rich, then I am being selfish. I am always amazed and amused by how people use and misuse words and by how readily people embrace the "love thy neighbor as thyself," admonition – which I think needs to be rephrased to "love thyself as thy neighbor."

I think most people are much nicer to, more compassionate toward, more understanding and forgiving of others than they are of themselves. The toughest boss I ever had during my entire career was me. I was relentless with myself and was so much kinder and more generous with others.

We are the most critical of ourselves, we demand the most from ourselves, and whenever we want to do something nice, or good or fun for ourselves, we think we are being selfish. Don't we deserve the same kindness and generosity of spirit from ourselves that we give to others?

And why shouldn't we do things for ourselves? What in the world is wrong with that? It's healthy and it fills us up with love and joy and overflowing abundance that spill over into everything we do and onto everyone we meet . . . so we become radiating centers of light and love.

Myth #11

I can't be rich because of my present circumstances,

my past history, my lack of education, the debt I am in, my children, and the list goes on and on.

When you read the 7 steps in this book and begin to understand how the universe really works – how we get what we want, what we expect and what we are willing to receive in life – when you begin to understand that *you*, not some outside force, circumstance or person determine your prosperity and the quality of your life; *you* determine everything you have, do or are; then you will become energized and empowered to create the life and the wealth you want . . . especially once you realize how simple and easy it really is to do.

Myth #12

I don't deserve to be rich. This simple, yet very pervasive belief is probably at the root of most people's circumstances and their current inability to create wealth and become rich.

You DO deserve to be rich. You deserve to have everything you want in life. It is your birthright. You were born to be rich . . . Claim it! And claim it with a feeling of entitlement. By entitlement, I do not mean arrogance, but rather a knowing, an expectation that what you are asking for is being given to you. Claim it with a grateful and humble heart in the knowing that all riches are yours for the asking, the taking, the enjoying and the sharing.

Claim it just as you do when you order something from a store or at a restaurant and don't wonder if it will be given to you. You know it will be because you've asked for it, so you expect it and wait for it to be delivered to you. You receive it graciously and willingly . . . in a relaxed and easy manner with no fear, doubts or anxiety about it.

Yes, you pay for those things. And in a way, you have already paid for your right to be rich – simply by being born and by being a human being. It is your inalienable right to pursue happiness in any way you want, as long as it is not harmful to others. If money makes you happy, if being rich helps you be happy, then it is your right to be and become rich . . . as rich as you want to be . . . and to enjoy it. You just need to ask for it.

That's how the universe works – we get what we ask for; we get what we expect; we get what we are ready, willing and able to allow into our lives. So now, the important thing is HOW we ask, and developing an awareness of WHAT we are really asking for.

So, let's get started. But before we do, let's completely obliterate any power those old myths may have by rewriting them as bold declarations that empower and energize us, because energy is what makes things happens, what sets things in motion . . . what activates your "on" switch.

CREATING NEW MYTHS TO CATAPULT YOU INTO WEALTH

Myth #1

IT IS NOBLE AND GOOD TO BE RICH AND HAVE LOTS OF MONEY.

Myth #2

IF I HAVE A LOT OF MONEY OR MORE THAN I NEED, I SET A GREAT EXAMPLE FOR OTHERS OF WHAT THEY CAN HAVE.

Myth #3

I AM THRILLED TO BE LIVING BETTER THAN MY PARENTS DID. I KNOW IT IS WHAT THEY WANT FOR ME.

Myth #4

RICH PEOPLE, LIKE ALL OTHER PEOPLE, ARE KIND, GENEROUS, FUN . . . AND HAVE LOTS OF SOUL AND DEPTH.

Myth #5

IF I AM RICH OR CARE ABOUT MONEY, I CAN ENJOY SO MANY SPIRITUAL THINGS AND GET TO LIVE ACCORDING TO MY DEEP-EST VALUES.

Myth #6

IF I CARE ABOUT MONEY, I GET TO ENJOY THINGS FOR THE AES-THETIC, SPIRITUAL, EMOTIONAL AND PHYSICAL PLEASURE THEY GIVE ME.

Myth #7

WANTING TO MAKE A LOT OF MONEY AND BE RICH IS A LOFTY, WORTHWHILE GOAL IN LIFE.

Myth #8

I CAN MAKE LOTS OF MONEY WITH EFFORTLESS EASE AND CAN ALSO MAINTAIN MY INTEGRITY AND VALUES.

Myth #9

THE EASIER THINGS ARE FOR ME, THE MORE GOD REJOICES.

Myth #10

IF I WANT A LOT OF MONEY AND WANT TO BE RICH, I AM BEING AS GOOD TO MYSELF AS I AM TO OTHER PEOPLE.

Myth #11

I HAVE THE POWER TO DETERMINE MY DESTINY – THE QUALITY OF MY LIFE AND WHAT I CAN DO, BE AND HAVE.

Myth #12

I DESERVE TO BE RICH.

"Be bold and mighty forces will come to your aid."

Basil King

2

STEP ONE

DECIDE

Yes, just *decide* to be rich! I know that sounds obvious
. . . and therefore perhaps a little crazy to tell you to *decide* to
be rich.

But it's not obvious. Most people do everything *but* decide
to be rich. They pray, they wish, they hope, they plead, they
beg, they make all kinds of bargains with and promises to God
if only he will make them rich. They *try* (more about that later)

all different things to get rich. But they don't make the decision to be rich.

We "humans" complicate everything so much that as we agonize over how to get rich, we wind up ignoring the one simple, very basic thing we all have to do that will unlock the door to becoming rich – and that is to *make the decision to be rich.*

Not that you 1) *want* to be rich, or that you 2) *wish* you *were* rich, or that you 3) *would like* to be rich – none of these is a decision. Not only are they not decisions – they are 1) hopeful and futuristic, and kind of watered down with little or no energy behind it 2) subjunctive, which implies an unreal situation 3) conditional, which is used when there are all kinds of qualifiers, conditions and parameters attached to a situation.

Most people avoid making a decision about almost everything in their lives . . . and don't even realize they are avoiding it . . . that they are being vague and non-committal. So many of us are not used to being declarative and decisive. It sounds so easy – just decide. But it isn't. Simple, yes; but not easy because "simple" is rarely easy for people. Our brains like to complicate things – and often we look for all kinds of convoluted answers and complex solutions to our prayers, questions and problems . . . and in so doing, we miss the very simple solution that is usually right there in front of us.

I remember two years ago when I was in Ottawa visiting a friend of mine. We were walking along the Rideau River, enjoying the varied and magnificent wildlife when I noticed a beautiful bird, with a shiny black coat and vibrant colors on its wings, perched on a stone wall. "That's a red-winged black-bird," my friend told me. Then he immediately turned around, looking for something. "Where's the other one?" he added. "They usually travel in pairs."

So, the two of us began looking all over the place for the second one – craning our necks, looking up and down, left and right – but we didn't see it anywhere. "Oh well," he said, "I guess there is only one this time." And we began to walk away.

Just then, I exclaimed, "Look! There it is!" Right there – perched on the stone wall directly in front of us, was the second red-winged blackbird we were looking for. It was right there in front of us all the time, but we were too busy looking for it everywhere else.

How often we miss the obvious that is so clear and simple and right in front of us . . . like just *deciding* to be rich.

HABITS

Most of us have unwittingly developed the habit of being indecisive, of procrastinating, of debating a subject endlessly in our minds (or with others); we are plagued by a whole host of "shoulds" and "should nots" and are generally so tentative, that *we don't even know what it really feels like to make a decision* – to commit unwaveringly to something . . . and therefore, we really don't understand the power that doing so wields.

Even marriage and relationships – how many people go into them with the thought, "Oh well, if it doesn't work out, I can always get divorced."

That attitude is deadly for any relationship or marriage. I was in a sixteen-year relationship and after the second year, I felt that it was never going to work out, so therefore, I was not going to commit to it . . . As a result, I never felt a strong need or desire to really try to work things out whenever problems arose.

Well, two years ago I was speaking with two friends of mine – a married couple celebrating their thirtieth anniversary. I knew she was a very volatile person who was difficult to live with and that there had been a lot of turmoil in their marriage. So I asked them, "Aren't you surprised that you made it to this point?"

"No, I'm not," her husband replied categorically – and he proceeded to explain something to me that has forever changed my entire perspective on commitment and the power of making a decision.

"During the first few years of our marriage," he said, "we argued constantly, and every time, Lisa would say, 'It looks like we're just going to have to get divorced.' This went on for a few years and the arguments got worse, until I made a decision. I decided that divorce was not an option for us. I decided that we were going to make this work. And I said to Lisa, 'Please don't ever mention divorce again. That is not an option. We are going to make this work!'"

"After that, everything changed for us. We began to look for solutions, rather than focusing on our problems. We began to see ourselves and work as a team, rather than adversaries. It was difficult, but we had made a decision and we were committed."

Wow! I – who have been commitment-phobic most of my life – thinking commitment meant limitation, resignation, the "end" – suddenly realized that quite the contrary . . . making a decision and being committed liberate you.

It takes so much energy to be indecisive, to straddle the fence, to walk in "Limbo" – and I even – for the first time – began to wonder if rather than me not making the decision to make my sixteen-year relationship work because I knew it wouldn't . . . perhaps, just perhaps the converse was true . . . that it didn't work because I never made the decision to make it work.

So – getting back to deciding to be rich . . . The very first thing you must do in your quest to be rich is to DECIDE TO BE RICH! It's that simple! Once you do this, everything . . . and I mean . . . *everything changes.*

Your decision repositions you – and your brain, your psyche, the universe start to look for ways for you to become rich . . . or to do, be or have whatever it is you have decided to.

They look for and create ways for you to make money and generate income, rather than wondering if you can. Your decision gets you looking forward, instead of backward. It moves you into the energy of possibility – an energy filled with anticipation and expectation rather than fear, worry and doubt.

Making a decision removes doubt, removes hesitation, removes all those stops and starts that hinder us and stop our forward momentum toward what we desire – the should I, could I, what if, why me, well maybe, I'll give it a try, how will I ever, and on and on *ad nauseum* with all those staccato melodies we play over and over in our minds. None of this exists any longer once you make a decision . . . instead, your energy and focus are now ahead, rather than on second-guessing yourself.

Once you decide to do, be or have something, an amazing thing happens. Your entire focus, perspective and standpoint shift – you are no longer hoping, wishing, fantasizing, dreaming, praying – instead you know, feel certain, see it, feel it, breathe it. It becomes real for you and you begin to live it . . . and therefore, make it happen.

I have found this with everything in my life – once I decide to do something – I just do it. The difficult part, the important thing, is deciding. But once you decide to do something – you can and will do it . . . you *will* find a way.

Perhaps that's why so many people hesitate to make decisions and find all sorts of excuses not to make a decision – because they know . . . on some subliminal level . . . the enormous responsibilities that come with making that decision. They know that those responsibilities will require them to stop being lazy, to move outside of their comfort zone, to change their habits and their lifestyle, and to welcome the new and the unknown . . . all of which is really scary.

They also find it scary to actually – for real – believe that they are about to get what they want. Believe it or not, many people say they want to be rich or famous or loved or happy or whatever, but deep down, they actually find the imminent possibility of getting what they want frightening, overwhelming, and intimidating. And they know, on some cellular level, that when they make a firm, unwavering decision, they will activate certain forces within and without them that will move them towards whatever it is they have decided to do, be or have and will simultaneously move whatever they have decided to do, be or have towards them . . . that they will set in motion and mobilize unseen forces working in their behalf . . . and that is scary.

Scary for so many reasons – people don't feel worthy, they are afraid they won't be able to handle it, they are afraid their lives will change, that they will lose their friends, that more will be required of them than they are willing or able to do . . . so they would rather stick with old, the familiar, the "known", even though it is not what or the life they want. At least they know that life, they know what they have and don't have and they are comfortable with what they know and do not find it so scary.

So ultimately, it is often fear . . . yes, fear of success that sometimes keeps people from deciding to be rich . . . or anything else they really want. It is fear that keeps them where they are. Fear . . . and laziness – the refusal, the unwillingness, the hesitation to change their habits, their patterns, their life.

THE FIELD OF ALL POSSIBILITIES

Making a decision, about anything, puts you in a state of readiness, preparedness and receptivity. You literally become a receptor for all the things, people and opportunities that can help you achieve what you want.

Making a decision catapults you into the energy of possibility where all things are possible because you have decided to allow them to be – you are inviting them into your life and experience.

Although you always reside in a state of unlimited potential . . . worry, fear, doubt, apprehension, hesitation – AND indecisiveness and ambiguity – hinder the smooth, easy, natural flow of that potential into your experience.

When you make a decision however, you welcome the field of all possibilities – literally like opening the door to let it in. All you have to do is be open, aware, receptive, flexible and responsive.

Hopefulness and wishful thinking are replaced by determination and focus on where you are going, rather than on where you are and where you have been. You step into a kind of certainty and a knowing – instead of a tentativeness. You start a process and create a momentum that propel you forward towards whatever it is you want.

WHERE ARE YOU GOING

I am reminded of the story of Christopher Columbus passionately recounted in Andy Andrews' book *The Traveler's Gift*. The main character who, through some time warp, lands aboard Columbus' ship, asks him, "Do you really not know where you are?" to which Columbus replies, (and I paraphrase) *No, but what does that matter? My whole life people have asked me that question about my station in life or what I am doing or what I think I can do. It matters not to me if I know where I am. What does matter is where I am going. Ask me that question. Ask me . . . Ask me where I am going!*

So, the main character asks Columbus, "Do you know where you are going?" to which Columbus thunderously replies, "Yes! Yes, I do know where I am going. I am going to the New World," which he proceeds to describe in vivid detail, even though he is not physically there yet and has never seen it. He tells the main character that tomorrow morning when the sun rises, land – the New World – will be right there in front of them, just where and as he has imagined it.

Einstein, perhaps the greatest physicist in the world, was also a great metaphysician. Even he said, "Imagination is more important than knowledge." Imagination allows us to *create* reality rather than waiting for it to happen and being mired in what *is*. He knew that the image becomes the reality (more about that in step 3).

WHEN, NOT IF

Once you make a firm, unwavering decision to be rich – the "if" literally slips out of the equation and it only becomes a matter of "when."

But you must make your decision to be rich with no ambiguity, no reservations, no guilt, no shame, no feelings of unworthiness or fears about not being spiritual or "noble" enough. No thoughts about "how" to accomplish it, "if" you can accomplish it. No thoughts about "why me?" but rather say . . . "Why not me!?"

Once you make your decision, you are catapulted into a whole new energy that is now mobilizing and looking for solutions and ways in which you can make money, attract people and things and opportunities into your life to help you.

You literally step out of the hypothetical world of "if" into the very real world of "when" – which starts attracting the "how" – often without your even working hard to discover the "how."

In fact, it is better if you don't work or think too hard because then you can become myopic, linear, anal and develop tunnel vision, like a horse with blinders on.

The whole beauty and wonder of this process of deciding to be rich (or successful or happy or anything, for that matter) is that it attracts and mobilizes resources from everywhere to help you achieve your goal – so you must be open, flexible, receptive and above all, be willing to think associatively . . . to see and make associations and connections between seemingly unrelated things so you can recognize and respond to opportunities when they arise.

For example, I remember when I had an advertising agency in Miami and one of my clients was a small resort condominium in Key West. At that time, a resort condominium was a brand new concept and we were not sure what would be the best way to advertise it with my client's limited budget.

During the time we were putting the ad campaign together, I read an interview in *Adweek* magazine with the Marketing Director of Coca Cola. In the interview, he spoke about the strategy they had used when they introduced Diet Coke. He said that at that time, diet soda was new and therefore, not widely popular or accepted. So any ad campaign they ran would first have to convince people to drink diet soda . . . and then, get them to drink Diet Coke. Rather than doing that, they decided to let their competition spend big money to first convince consumers to drink diet soda . . . Once that was accomplished, then Coca Cola stepped in with a big ad campaign for Diet Coke.

Voilà . . . we had our answer. We did not spend my client's limited advertising budget promoting them as a resort condominium, (most people didn't even know what a resort condominium was then) . . . Instead, we promoted it simply as a resort. Then once we got tourists and vacationers to visit or stay at the property, we made them aware of the condominium option.

Associative thinking is definitely an asset once you make a decision to do something . . . especially since deciding to be rich . . . or anything else you want to do, be or have magnetizes anything you want or need to help you accomplish what you want. So thinking associatively multiplies your options and opportunities exponentially.

Making up your mind to do something is like the organizing principle that allows everything to happen and fall into place . . . like a kaleidoscope organizes the myriad pieces inside into all different patterns.

Without making a decision however, nothing can happen, unless literally, as a result of blind luck – which does occur occasionally.

But if you want something . . . anything – to have money, to find your soul-mate, to be a better parent, to do work that you love, to be happy . . . anything – all you have to do is decide to do, be or have it . . . and you will because your decision lays the foundation and creates a place for it to come into your life.

Like in the film *Field of Dreams*. Although the movie is a fantasy, it illustrates an essential principle of the universe – if you create a space for something, decide to have it, and then expect it, wait for it, prepare for it . . . it will come, without fail. Maybe not always in the form you expect or think it will . . . for our thinking is often so limited and often too small and narrow . . . but it will surely come to fill up the space you have created for it.

All you have to do is decide . . . Decide to be rich . . . Decide to be happy . . . Decide to be healthy . . . Just Decide . . . whatever it is you want . . . decide to be it, have it, do it . . . and you will.

WHY DOES THIS WORK?

Why? Because we live in a friendly universe that is always for us. When I say the universe is "always for us," I do not mean that it likes you. That would imply judgment and subjectivity, and the universe is totally impersonal and objective. Therefore, it is as much for you as it is for anyone else. There is no favoritism or partiality.

Why is the universe friendly? Because it is. Years ago, I was with my cousin's daughter and her four-year old son who kept doing something his mother repeatedly kept telling him not to do. Finally, he looked up at her and simply asked, "Why?" And she replied, without any hesitation – "Because I'm the mommy." I thought that was a great answer!

So why is the universe a friendly place? Because it is. It is benevolent and conducive to the growth and blossoming of all kinds of plants and wildlife; the procreation and survival of a plethora of animals; the creation of incredible natural wonders like the Grand Canyon, trees, the sky and autumn; and miraculous wonders like the flight of the Bumble Bee, people being able to fly, and a Hummingbird being able to stop in mid-air. So why shouldn't it be friendly to us?

Why is the universe a friendly place? Because why create something . . . an entire world . . . and not have it be friendly? It just doesn't make sense.

Why is the universe a friendly place? Because it functions according to natural laws – and when those laws are recognized and incorporated into a life, the universe *must* respond in a certain way. It has no choice.

Why does it work? Because everything is energy. The great thinkers of all ages have told us that in one way or another – from Plato to Einstein to the Dalai Lama to Deepak Chopra. Everything in the world, including us, is merely a field of energy and information. How we choose to organize, use and manifest that energy and information is up to us. It is not predetermined – *We* choose who we want to be, how we want to live. And we do this by the choices we make. We decide what we get, have, do and experience in life.

And since the world is a mirror – literally a reflective mirror of energy – what we put out is what we get back. The energy we put into the world is reflected back at us in our experience. And in that way, it really is true that we get what we give. This is not some abstract metaphysical theory, but an observable fact and law of nature.

Perhaps you have heard the expression "Like attracts like." Well, it's true. Have you ever noticed that when you are angry, disgruntled or dissatisfied, everything seems to go wrong and you seem to be surrounded by people with problems and complaints?

And when you are happy, generous and feeling abundant and full of love, you find yourself "in the zone," with every-thing going right, things just falling into place and in the company of happy, loving, contented people.

So since everything is energy, deciding to be rich or happy, magnetizes rich and happy people, situations and experiences to you. All you have to do is be ready and respond.

DO . . . NOT TRY

In *The Empire Strikes Back*, the second film in the *Star Wars* saga, George Lucas has the wise sage Yoda give the young Luke Skywalker some advice. He tells Luke to:

"Try not . . . Do or do not . . . There is no try."

This advice is absolutely invaluable. "Try" is a word that I believe should be banished from the English language. It has been the excuse, the crutch, the "out" for so many people . . . for so many things in their lives.

Once you say "I'll try," you are doomed to fail. Trying is half-hearted. Trying implies that if it doesn't work out or you don't succeed, at least you tried.

Not good enough! Not for something you really want or care about.

Trying is only productive when it is used to experiment or experience something new . . . but never, never to be used to refer to something you really, deeply, truly desire.

Why doesn't trying work? Because it has no energy to it. Trying, by definition, lacks real passion and commitment – the two things that are absolutely necessary to create momentum.

Momentum is ignited by a decision. (More about that in step 2.) By deciding, you activate your "on" switch, the "enter" mode, the "yes" button . . . *yes* I am ready, *yes* I can, *yes* I will, *yes* I do . . . *yes I am yes I can yes I will yes . . . yes . . . yes . . .*

That readiness fosters a sense of entitlement . . . Entitlement, not as arrogance, but as a readiness and a willingness to accept and receive what it is you are asking for . . . Entitlement as the willingness to even ask for what you what . . . and then to expect it.

I remember when I was working as a Media Director at a small advertising agency in Miami. It was my first job in advertising after being an instructor at the university, and I knew nothing about advertising, so my boss hired me at an appallingly low salary (especially for a single mother with responsibilities).

As I learned the industry and got better at my job, which I did very quickly, I would go into my boss's office and ask for a raise . . . and I always got it – about four or five times in the two and a half years I worked there.

The interesting thing is that as I look back, I realize that I never really went in to "ask" for a raise . . . it was more like, "OK, I'm ready now. You can give me a raise."

Interesting isn't it? That's the same psychology and perspective you need to come from when you "ask" to be rich . . . that you are not asking at all, but rather, announcing that you are ready to be rich, you are willing to be rich . . . that you have made up your mind to be rich.

THE UNIVERSAL CATALOG

As I said, I got every raise I "asked" for.

An interesting aside about that . . . and a story I've repeatedly told my son . . . is that the receptionist/bookkeeper, who was very good at her job and actually friends with our boss, never received a raise.

Finally one day, exasperated, she went into the owner of the agency and confronted him. "Why is Madeleine always getting raises and I'm not?" He paused a moment, reflected and said, "Because she asks me."

It's as simple as that! How amazing how often we overlook the obvious. You have to ask for what you want . . . and you have to be ready for it . . . willing and able to receive it whole-heartedly, unabashedly and categorically. You have to feel like you deserve it.

We all get what we ask for – literally, almost like ordering out of a catalog. Except in a catalog, things are displayed right there for us, so we know what we are ordering.

In our lives however, most of us either don't really realize what we are asking for; or we don't really directly ask for anything in particular, not clearly and distinctly and passionately and unwaveringly; or we keep changing our minds and then wonder why we don't get what we want; or we are ambiguous and ambivalent.

Most people don't even really know what they want. They know what they *don't* want, but not what they *do* want. But knowing what you don't want will not get you what you do want because knowing what you don't want has you looking in the wrong direction – backwards instead of forward. It has you saying "no" instead of "yes." It has you in a state of dissatisfaction rather than anticipation.

PUSH AND PULL

Anais Nin, an extraordinary diarist who was good friends with Henry Miller in 1920's Paris, wrote in her Third (and I believe, her best) Diary:

> *"And the day came when the risk to remain tight in a*
> *bud was more painful than the risk it took to blossom."*

It is the "pull" that attracts us, that calls to us, that ignites our passion and liberates an endless store of energy inside us.

The "push" only causes resistance, sluggishness and drains our energy.

I am reminded of a story Norman Vincent Peale (I believe it was him) wrote of growing up on a farm. One day, a storm was coming and both his father and grandfather rushed to get the cows (or was it the horses?) into the barn before the storm hit.

They got behind the animals and pushed and pushed, but couldn't get them to budge. The more they pushed, the more the animals resisted. Watching this, Peale, then a young boy, learned a valuable lesson. Finally, he asked his father and grandfather if he could try. Exasperated with their dismal efforts, they said, "Sure."

So Peale got behind the lead animal, pulled its tail . . . it bolted right into the barn and all the other animals followed.

It's what pulls us toward it that motivates us and gives us energy. A decision made to move toward something is always more productive and energizing than a decision made to move away from something.

Know this . . . that once you make up your mind . . . about anything . . . there is no stopping you. Why? Because you strip yourself and the situation down to the bare essentials . . . you distill everything down to the very core of what works, what you need to do to get whatever you want.

Once you make up your mind and make a decision, you eliminate the extraneous and the hypothetical . . . so that the reality of what you desire becomes a *fait accompli*. Then it is only a matter of time until the external reality you are experiencing will catch up with and mirror your inner reality.

WHAT INTERFERES WITH
MAKING A DECISION

- Laziness
- Ignorance (don't even realize you haven't made or need to make a decision)
- Habit
- Reluctance to move out of your comfort zone
- Fear
- Avoidance of responsibility that comes with getting, being, doing, having what you desire.

Fear has energy. Don't resist your fear.
Use that energy and transmute it.

Change the fear and avoidance of the new
and the unknown to excitement.

Realize that boredom is draining,
risk is energizing.

Choose to step into what energizes you,
excites you and vitalizes you.

Embrace the new and the unknown as
extraordinary presents, just waiting
for you to unwrap them.

THINGS YOU CAN DO TO HELP YOU DECIDE

- Replace the word "if" with "when."

- Do . . . don't try.

- Forget about what you don't want. Concentrate only on what you DO want. (There is a Swiss custom of filling up and tossing a big bowl of water out of every door in your house for the New Year. This gets rid of all the old things you do not want and ushers in a clean, fresh New Year. You might want to try this. It's simple and anyone can do it.)

- Since "nature abhors a vacuum," once you get rid of what you don't want, you need to fill the space with what you do want. You can write it down, or just think about, dream, declare, or do some activities that exemplify the "you" and the life you do want.

- Begin *savoring* your life . . . not just working at it. Begin *savoring* getting rich . . . not just struggling to. Begin the process of becoming *deliciously* rich . . . not just filthy or obscenely rich.

ACTION TIPS - STEP 1

There is only one thing you need to do . . .

DECIDE to be rich . . . or whatever else you want.

*D*o whatever it takes, whatever you have to do to get clear, focused and determined. Decide what you want and decide to be it, have it, do it or get it. Make up your mind and then expect it, welcome it, prepare for it, get excited about it . . . and know it is on its way.

Claude Bristol, author of a wonderful little book titled The Magic of Believing, tells the story of when he landed in France in 1918 as a "casual soldier," unattached to a regular company.

Although his basic needs were taken care of by the Army, he found himself with no money "to buy gum, candy, cigarettes and the like. Every time I saw a man light a cigarette or chew a stick of gum, the thought came that I was without money to spend on myself.

. . . I grew bitter because I had no spending money and no way of getting any. One night en route to the forward area on a crowded troop train when sleep was out of the question, I made up my mind that when I returned to civilian life, 'I would

have a lot of money.' The whole pattern of my life was altered at that moment."

. . . .

*If there is something **you** want in your life that you do not now have – whether it's money, a mate, a job you love, children, happiness, good health . . . whatever it is . . . make up your mind now to have it . . . and forever alter your life in this moment.*

"What you can do, or dream you can, do it;
Boldness has genius, power and magic in it."

Johann Wolfgang von Goethe

3

STEP TWO

ACT

*D*o something . . . Anything. Just get started . . . even with the seemingly smallest thing.

Don't wait until all conditions are perfect or everything is in place. They will never be. If you wait until they are, the time will never be right and you will never begin – because there will always be some new thing, something else . . . a small little detail that is not the way you want it to be.

So just jump in and do it . . . do it now.

Mark Burnett, the executive producer of such hit shows as *Survivor* and *The Apprentice* practically "invented" reality TV and revolutionized television in general.

How did he do it? How did this British immigrant who came to this country with very little money and absolutely no knowledge of the entertainment industry and no connections to or with anyone create his own entertainment empire ... in a relatively short time?

By jumping in with both feet, seizing the moment, taking risks and daring to think big in his pursuit of success.

When Burnett first came to the States, this former British army paratrooper was on his way to South America, but decided to stay in California instead. Finding himself with practically no money and knowing no one, he took a job as a nanny (Yes – a nanny!) to a big Hollywood mogul and his family.

He worked as a nanny for two years – during which time he saw how he wanted to live and became firm in his resolve to someday live that life ... in fact, he decided to even live on that same street someday.

When he quit being a nanny, he began to sell t-shirts on Venice Beach – and saved enough money from both his endeavors to buy a small piece of real estate ... sold it, made some money ... and began to build his empire and live his dream. (By the way, he did eventually – within just a few years – not only live on that same street, but in the very same house, which he bought from his former boss.)

So not only is it imperative to act – to do something, (the action you take can be small, seem trivial, appear totally unrelated to whatever it is you want – like being a nanny or selling t-shirts is to becoming a producer), but nothing . . . not even the seemingly most bizarre action . . . can ever be ruled out as unimportant.

In meteorology, there is a theory called "The Butterfly Effect," which states that a butterfly flapping its wings off the coast of Africa can cause a hurricane in the Atlantic.

Since everything and everyone is connected in this web of life, (Chief Seattle tells us that "We are all part of the web of life. What we do to the web, we do to ourselves"), if you just begin, if you act . . . and keep on "acting" and "doing," eventually you will wind up where you want to be – often even surpassing your original vision.

PUTTING ON YOUR DIRECTIONAL

I once heard a quote that said, "If you continue heading in the direction you are going, that is where you will end up." It sounds obvious when it's verbalized, but in our actions, it isn't so obvious. Sometimes we continue doing the same thing over and over expecting different results; we continue heading in a certain direction even though we want to go in an entirely different direction.

For example, so many people say they want to be rich, they want to live a certain lifestyle, yet every day, they continue to only associate with the same people they always have who are in the same rut they are in, participate in activities toward which these same people gravitate and shop at and frequent the same places they always have, with the same people they always have.

If you want to rise to a new level – whether it is financial, intellectual, social, or cultural – you must expose yourself to and begin to associate and mingle with people who have already reached that level. You need to go to, frequent or shop at those places that attract those people and embody that life-style and level to which you aspire. It's a way of tricking your psyche and your body into believing and beginning to act like those people you desire to live like.

So, making a decision to do something points you in the right direction and turns on your ignition . . . and acting, or doing something, actually puts you in gear. The rest is all process, according to a basic law of the universe – *If the first 15% of anything is done correctly, the remaining 85% will fall into place with relative ease.*

And deciding and acting are the two things that constitute the first 15%. If you can and will make a firm, unwavering com-mitment to be rich, (or to do, be or have whatever it is you want) . . . and then act on that decision, you begin to set in motion a process that will eventually lead you to what you desire.

CARPE DIEM

Acting – doing something – is simple, so don't complicate it. Don't get stuck in your mind with deliberations about "should I," "can I," "is it appropriate," "will it lead me to my desired goal." None of those questions matters – and in fact, if you begin deliberating, they will probably hamper you in your pursuit of success.

Why? For so many reasons.

Action that is taken in the moment, while the spark of passion and enthusiasm is lit, is fueled with a momentum and a propulsion that action that is filtered through the often agonizing, laborious and paralyzing deliberation process is not. Once your mind and mental filters enter the process, so does the critic, the censor, the editor, the judge . . . and they open the door to fear, doubt, procrastination and hesitation.

Now I am not suggesting that anyone act frivolously, foolishly or irresponsibly. In fact, getting back to the original definition of responsible – which means "able to respond" (not react . . . but respond. There is a huge difference), I believe that our physiology (our mind/body) has a built-in mechanism that knows when we are ready for something, when we are able to do what it is we want, when we are able to respond organically from within rather than react to something that is without or outside of us . . . and that mechanism inside us is what helps light that spark . . . That spark is simply the spontaneous combustion caused by the meeting of readiness and opportunity.

And if we start thinking too much, that spark diminishes . . . that electrical current gets short-circuited . . . and the moment is lost. And then we must wait for another moment . . . prepare to ignite another spark. But if we keep "short-circuiting" those sparks – those moments – eventually they will come less and less frequently, until eventually, they become like buried cable wires that we have to dig deep to get to, which then takes a huge amount of effort.

A friend of mine, who has always been obsessed with money and fearful of all change, the unknown and any new experience – especially those involving money – was no longer happy, since she retired, living in the same house or neighborhood she had been living in and really wanted to change her life.

An opportunity arose for her to sell her house at a huge profit and move, but she was terrified of moving, of making any change or decision. She didn't sleep nights; spent every waking hour worrying, afraid and depressed; spent hours crying on the phone as I kept urging her to "just do it." To just list the house with a realtor . . . assuring her that once she did that, once she made the decision and acted on it . . . everything would change. I assured her that the mere fact of her taking some action would rearrange her life, her energy, her perspective and her priorities completely . . . and catapult her into the forward-moving energy of anticipation, excitement and things to do, rather than her present energy of fear and paralysis that were focusing on the security she thought she was losing.

Well, she listened to me, and the instant . . . literally, the instant she listed the house with a realtor, everything changed. Not only did she become involved in all the details necessitated by her action in preparing the house for sale, looking for a new house, packing, etc. . . . she had finally broken through her lifelong paralyzing fear . . . and totally, totally transformed her life from that day forward.

The energy it took for her to be so afraid was finally released and she became a risk-taker who now has investment properties, tries new things, and is generally quite free-spirited and unafraid – a totally different person who is happier, freer, and much richer.

BODY LANGUAGE

When you act on your decision to be rich (or anything else), readiness is essential. Not readiness as in everything being in place – but readiness in terms of your being congruent within yourself – in what you want, what you have decided to have and are really ready to receive, and what you believe you can and will have (more about that in step 3).

So readiness is really a threshold upon which you stand . . . and a portal through which you are ready to walk in order to claim what it is you desire.

An integral part of readiness means getting to know and trust your intuition and your body – because when you are ready, when something is right, you will feel it in your body. It will just feel right . . . and you will know; your body never lies.

But this feeling is subtle – and requires that you begin to tune into your body, to feel it and trust it. Begin to notice those feelings in the pit of your stomach, or in your throat, or those voices that spur you on or tell you to wait. It's different for everyone . . . but everybody's body dialogues with them; everybody's body knows what's right for them and uses different methods to communicate with them. So tune into how and where your body communicates with you . . . learn to listen to it . . . and eventually . . . to trust it.

Start with small things first – like should I go to that lecture tonight or should I go to the dance class? Should I turn left or right to find a parking space? As you tune into this dialogue with small things, you will begin to trust the "knowingness" of your mind/body for larger, more important things.

Every successful business entrepreneur and all great thinkers have more often relied on their intuition and "gut" feelings than deliberative reasoning, from Donald Trump to Einstein. In fact, Trump, in his book, *The Art of the Deal*, talks about making decisions quickly, intuitively and acting on them immediately.

ACT AND WORK SMARTER, NOT HARDER

Throughout financial, business and even, metaphysical circles, there is a widely known and accepted theory called the 80/20 Theory. Quite simply, this theory states that 80% of our time and energy are spent on things that only generate 20% of our income, while most of us spend only 20% of our time and energy on those things that generate and are responsible for 80% of our income.

The old work ethic of working hard is not necessarily the most effective way to get what you want. Working smarter is infinitely more effective . . . and a lot more satisfying than working hard.

Which brings me back to energy . . . the energy with which you act. When you act immediately and quickly, your action is infused with passion, gusto, vitality and a kind of laser-like quality and focus . . . with an energy that has the ability to mobilize resources, propel you forward, create momentum, and radiate a magnetic energy out into the world around you to touch, communicate with and ultimately attract to you everything you need to fulfill your desires.

It is the passion, enthusiasm and excitement with which you act that makes you unstoppable . . . that enable you to get more done in a short period of time, and to do it better, more effectively, efficiently, and with effortless ease . . . and . . . to even have fun while doing it.

Let me interject here that the word "act" is not used in a singular sense. It is used as a collective, cumulative, continuous term. For it is essential that you continue to act – to do things, instead of just thinking about them or planning for them.

In most cases, I have found, that planning is often an excuse for not beginning, for not doing . . . and planning often drags out endlessly until it smothers, dampens and dulls any excitement, enthusiasm and passion one might have had, making the thing you wanted to do a monumental task because you have sucked all the life, energy and momentum out of it

. . . and you yourself have been reduced to a stand-still – stuck in the quicksand of inertia.

Most people don't realize however, that the word "inertia" has a double meaning – "An object in motion will stay in motion and an object at rest will remain at rest until an opposite action is applied to change that."

Most people usually only focus on the latter and think "inertia" means being stuck, not moving, unable to get started.

But the positive flip side of inertia is that once you have started to move and are in motion, if you remain in motion, then progress and movement will remain relatively easy. But once you stop, then you enter the negative side of inertia – and will stay at rest and immobile until something gets you moving again . . . and it will take much more effort for you to start over from a stand-still position than it would have taken for you to just continue moving once you were already in motion.

That's why the first 15% of anything you do is so important. Once you decide what you want and act on that decision, you have mobilized the positive force of inertia – you have set things and yourself in motion. Then all you need to do is stay in motion . . . and this is usually accomplished with relatively little effort.

Claude Bristol writes that ". . . persistence gives confidence and continued right mental attitude followed by consistent action will bring success." Persistence does build confidence. Every time you do something, you feel empowered . . . no matter how small that action is. So the benefits of each action become cumulative and feed the next one.

And consistent action does not mean sequential action at all. It means continuous action. Every day, do something. Just keep moving forward . . . keep doing things that feel right. Sometimes these things will seem to make no sense at all (as I am sure being a nanny did not to Mark Burnett at the outset). But eventually, a pattern will emerge. Just be willing to be open, diversified and flexible . . . because life is lived and experienced associatively, not linearly . . . so our plans, hopes and dreams are fed by many different and divergent tributaries . . . and we never know from which source something wonderful and serendipitous will emerge.

So rather than your actions being linear or sequential, it is far more important that they be self-contained – in the moment. Rather than acting based on seeing each act as the next step in the direction of or toward your desired goal, it is more important to be fully present in each action, to be committed to and focused on and in each action so there are no distractions and none of your energy is dissipated . . . and the benefits are therefore, multiplied exponentially.

So "act" does not mean to go into full implementation immediately. It doesn't mean to start planning. It means to begin taking action . . . to ask questions . . . to begin the treasure hunt with an open and expectant heart . . . to begin connecting the dots with a patience and a knowing that the full picture will emerge.

THE DOMINO EFFECT

Things really started to happen for me only once I *decided* to be rich . . . and actually did something about it. I began to do things differently than I did before. I began to do things where previously, I hadn't done anything.

Suddenly, I began meeting people who were staggeringly wealthy and influential, who invited and welcomed me into their circle, and I began to enjoy not only a glimpse into, but also a taste of what that life I wanted for myself was like.

I was invited to speak at a major fund raiser for a children's non-profit that a reader of mine started after reading my book, *Living Serendipitously . . . keeping the wonder alive.* There I mingled with the powerful and upper echelon members of society and politics and luxuriated in five-star Old World hotel accommodations, amenities and treatment that is usually reserved only for VIP's.

Seemingly out of nowhere, suddenly business and creative opportunities, that had been available to me all along, began opening up and materializing and coming to fruition quickly, easily and with almost no effort at all. I began doing things I never had before – writing e-books, offering e-courses and teleseminars, speaking and consulting more.

I began doing a lot more mentoring and coaching in the entire spectrum of all of my areas of expertise, instead of just the more limited areas I had been focusing on. I began coaching and mentoring programs to reach and help more people, while building a private, very lucrative and extremely satisfying coaching and mentoring practice with select clients.

I developed and expanded my company and interests, which I had wanted to do for awhile, into areas I had only dreamed of before – *The Living Serendipitously Institute* and *Living Serendipitously Enterprises* – offering products and services I love and developing new ones I had been wanting to; partnering with other experts and people I'd admired in joint ventures and projects.

Even something as remote as getting my dog into commercials and movies happened. While I was away in Chicago, a casting agent had seen my neighbor walking my dog and went "crazy over him" and said he wanted to cast him in film and on TV . . . and *voilà*, a star was born . . . and an exciting new venture for me that's been both fun and profitable.

It's all been so serendipitous . . . so absolutely plentiful and abundant . . . literally like a cornucopia of offerings, opportunities, chance meetings and synchronistic events ever since I *decided*, really *decided* to be rich . . . and began to *do* something about it.

Once I began acting and doing things, it was literally like opening some magical door out of which spilled more and more and more. It was almost as though I had turned on some switch and released a storehouse of riches there for the offering . . . just waiting for me to claim them – a supreme and undeniable confirmation of the principal that "Abundance is not something we acquire. It is something we tap into." It is already there. It already exists in the universe, which is plentiful and limitless. We just have to tap into it – just like turning on a light switch to allow the electrical current to flow through to the light.

And this prosperity . . . this abundance is available to everyone who is willing and ready to tap into it . . . willing to just *do* something . . . anything . . . to initiate the flow.

ACT OUT OF A DESIRE FOR MORE

I recently became acquainted with a woman who came to me for some writing coaching and mentoring. She told me how happily married she was for thirty years . . . and then her husband died. For two years, she stayed home alone and was achingly lonely, until one day, she decided she wanted more out of life.

At the same time, a gentleman in a completely other part of the country, who had lost his wife two years earlier, was also withering away and wallowing in depression and loneliness, until he decided that he had a choice. He could live or he could die . . . and he decided to live. So he began going to the gym, got himself in shape, and when he felt healthier, better and was ready, he booked a cruise to some exotic destination in Africa . . . the same cruise on which this woman had booked passage.

Well, just like out of one of those cinematic sweeping sagas, they met, fell in love, married, and – for seventeen years – shared an exotic, exciting life and the kind of romantic love you only read about . . . *And* they were filthy, obscenely . . . deliciously rich too! And all because each of them decided to *do* something . . . to take some action on their decision to get more out of life.

So acting, making one small or large gesture, can change everything. The important thing is to act . . . to *do* something . . . which sets in motion a chain of events that take on a life of their own . . . and you never know where they will lead you.

So when you do act, always operate and act out of desire, not need. Need focuses on lack, the thing you don't have, what you don't want. Desire focuses on what you do want and attracts it to you . . . and will therefore guide you to the right decision. Then just believe . . . and wait for and expect it to happen.

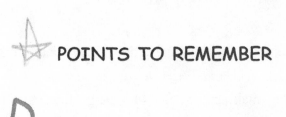
POINTS TO REMEMBER

*D*o something . . . anything. Even if it turns out to be not the best action to have taken, at least you did something. You began . . . and that is empowering and initiates a momentum.

Do it now. Do it while you feel some passion, some excitement, some enthusiasm.

Don't think, deliberate or plan. Jump in.

Go with your "gut" feeling and trust your intuition.

Follow up one action with another and then another and then another . . . and soon it will become second nature as the momentum carries you along and you feel comfortable in your new *modus operandi.*

ACTION TIPS - STEP 2

1. Now that you have decided to be rich (or whatever else you want), think of one thing you can do to achieve that goal . . . and then do it. Take one action on it. See how good it makes you feel. How empowering it is.

2. Now take another action and another. Each day, do at least one thing that moves you closer to what you want and experience how energizing that is . . . and how each action, no matter how small, motivates you to take another and another and another. Then, just keep that momentum going with small, incremental (sometimes lateral) actions, the purpose of which is to just keep you in motion. You will notice that no matter how small your steps, they will multiply exponentially and often mushroom into huge, wonderful consequences and opportunities.

3. Get a copy of Mark Burnett's book, *Jump In . . . Even If You Don't Know How to Swim* and read it. It's a fast, easy read that you can even skim. It's more the energy of the book that I'm interested in you experiencing, than any particular information, although reading how he accomplished what he did will certainly inspire and motivate you . . . and get you to realize that you can do anything you want – and you can begin to do it now – right where you are.

4. Honestly assess where you are now – what your strengths, talents, interests, assets are now – and begin from there. Don't try to "reinvent the wheel." Start with what you have, know and are good at and are perhaps, even doing to some degree already . . . and use that as your launching point.

   Once you begin making money, you can always expand or change what you are doing if you want. For now, just get started in the easiest, simplest, most expeditious way possible. Focus in on what you want to develop and can do easily and quickly to begin generating immediate income. You can always build on it later.

5. Do something fun . . . Go dancing, see a zany comedy, get together with a friend and laugh. Don't think or talk about any of this.

6. Go someplace wealthy people normally go or do something affluent people do. Put yourself in their circle and mingle with them. Go with the feeling that you belong there and put yourself in the place and position to meet some . . . a least one rich, influential person. Even if you don't meet anyone this first time, you will feel differently about yourself just being there and doing that.

   Some suggestions – Visit Cartier or some high priced clothing or jewelry store and let the store personnel wait on you as a potential customer; browse a model home in a very upscale new development and ask questions, get brochures, inquire about cost and amenities, always thinking of yourself and feeling like you are there to one day buy if you choose to. Lose yourself in the experience. Be there totally. Be fully present and always with the belief that you deserve to be there and belong.

7. Practice hearing and listening to your body when it tells you something feels right or does not feel right. Start with something small at first like deciding which street to turn down to find a parking space; or the next time you go shopping, notice if you are making a frivolous purchase, how it feels in your body . . . if it feels like you should make the purchase or not. Once you learn to hear, listen to and trust what I call your "body language," you can begin to develop that dialogue, rapport and trust with larger, more important things.

8. And finally, determine your own 80/20 factor. Figure out what you are spending 80% of your time on that is giving you only a 20% return . . . and then figure out what you need to spend only 20% of your time on that will give you an 80% return. Most of the time, it is just a matter of no longer busying yourself with endless errands and allowing yourself and your time to be consumed by trivial, unimportant things that keep you busy, but sap your energy and get you nowhere.

It is also a matter of taking the time to think about the 80/20 factor and focusing on what you need to do that will give you the most immediate and largest return for the least amount of effort and time. THAT is working smarter, rather than harder. All the people of great accomplishment do that . . . they work smart, not necessarily hard. Which doesn't mean they don't work hard, but when you are working smart, when you are going with your energy flow, the work seems like play and is so much easier . . . It just flows . . . and you accomplish more with effortless ease.

. . . .

AND REMEMBER TO LIVE SERENDIPITOUSLY . . .
ENJOY . . . PROSPER . . .
AND DARE TO BE RICH!

"They can because they think they can."

Virgil

4

STEP THREE

Believe

*T*hey can because they *believe* they can. But even that does not say it all because the words "think" and "believe" have come to be so limited and limiting in our modern culture.

We have overused these phrases so much, that they have become largely one-dimensional phrases (at best – 1½ dimensional, when you add some feeling to belief) that get stuck in our minds and rarely go beyond our mental processes which by themselves, rarely accomplish what we desire, and often even, confuse, hamper and interfere with our getting what we desire.

The impetus and the fuel for achieving our desires come from something other than our mind. Our mind is often cluttered, unfocused, overwhelmed and has to be controlled by something more powerful, more focused, more unstoppable than the mind – and that is our will . . . or our spirit . . . or that "thing" inside us that drives us; what Dylan Thomas calls "thru the green fuse drives the flower."

It is that "thing," that "force" inside us – that mental process infused with faith and passion – that makes all things possible and real to us even when everything appears to indicate the opposite.

A STORY

Again, I am reminded of the story of Christopher Columbus – a story I never thought much about my entire life. I just remember learning in grade school that Columbus discovered America, and that was the end of it.

But now, as an adult with a deep awareness and appreciation of the miracles we can achieve with our will, our power of belief – I am awed by the story of Christopher Columbus – which was brought to life for me so clearly by what Andy Andrews wrote in his book *The Traveler's Gift*, in

which a modern man named David, travels though time and
lands on Columbus's ship with him.

*For nineteen years, I endured the agony of public
humiliation for my convictions." [Columbus said]*

"Which convictions?" David asked.

*"The conviction . . ." Columbus said, his voice rising,
"no, the absolute certainty that I can establish a new
trade route by sailing west. West!"*

*Columbus grabbed David by the shoulders and
shook him once as he said, "My friend! The world
is a sphere! It is not flat! We are sailing around the
earth on the smooth surface of a sphere. We will not
fall off some imaginary edge!"*

*"Are you the only person who believes this?" David
asked.*

*"At the moment, yes," Columbus said, "but that
bothers me not in the least. Truth is truth. If a
thousand people believe something foolish, it is still
foolish! Truth is never dependent upon consensus
of opinion. I have found that it is better to be alone
and acting upon the truth in my heart than to follow
a gaggle of silly geese doomed to mediocrity."*

"You say it doesn't bother you in the least," David said. "You don't care that people think you are . . . well . . . crazy?"

"My friend," Columbus said with a smile, "if you worry about what other people think of you, then you will have more confidence in their opinion than you have in your own. Poor is the man whose future depends on the opinions and permission of others. Remember this, if you are afraid of criticism, you will die doing nothing!"

David frowned. "But with so many people against you," he asked, "how did you get started in the first place?"

"Getting started, getting finished – both ends of a journey require a demonstration of passion." Columbus mused. David stared blankly at the great man. "Passion!" he said again in a forceful whisper. "Passion is a product of the heart. Passion is what helps you when you have a great dream. Passion breeds conviction and turns mediocrity into excellence!

Your passion will motivate others to join you in pursuit of your dream. With passion, you will overcome insurmountable obstacles. You will become unstop-pable!"

That is the kind of belief I am talking about when I say "belief" is the third step in becoming rich or getting anything you want. I am talking about belief as faith . . . belief as trust . . . belief that is rooted in passion and such conviction that it becomes a knowing. I am talking about a belief that inhabits you so completely, that the reality of it, the accomplishment of it, the "living" of it is never in question.

This kind of belief radiates out from the believer and acts as a magnetic field as well as a laser. So not only does it magnetize to you everything and everyone you need to achieve your desired goal, it also keeps you focused, so that it is often not even necessary to consciously make an effort and mentally think of the "how" as you move inexorably toward what you want.

Yes – *inexorably* – what a fabulous word! It captures the essence of that process this kind of belief initiates and sustains. Webster defines *inexorable* as "not to be stopped by entreaty of any kind; relentless."

FULL- BODIED BELIEF

So when you have this kind of "full-bodied" belief, you cannot be dissuaded, stymied or seduced by any form of entreaty – not by doubts, questions, not even pleading. You literally become unstoppable . . . and you *will* reach your desired goal – guaranteed!

This kind of belief is literally like jet propulsion fuel – it propels you directly to your goal. This kind of belief has you doing, not trying. This kind of belief has you always moving forward, not looking backward. In fact, you don't have time or any inclination to ever look back, to hesitate or to doubt . . . all of which literally become unthinkable in the respect that they are so alien, so foreign, that they never even enter your mind.

So, I am not talking about "positive thinking." I am referring instead, to something much more powerful, much more pervasive . . . I am talking about what I call *full-bodied possibility living*. It is not just a mental attitude that you have in your mind; it is a belief that you "embody." It lives and breathes in every cell of your body, so of course, it becomes real.

Of course, the belief becomes the reality. The "belief-thought" creates the form or the material object or reality because it is a full-bodied, three-dimensional (actually four or five-dimensional) belief that is infused with your passion, desire, unwavering faith, and trust . . . with an unshakable certainty.

Out of the box

This kind of certainty arises only when we are willing to get "out of our minds." I know that phrase sounds scary. When I was growing up, "out of your mind" meant that you were crazy.

But I begin to wonder more and more if when the phrase originated, it meant something totally different. If perhaps it didn't refer to someone who was willing to go beyond the boundaries of the rational mind that analyzes and reacts to things based on what it perceives with our five senses. If perhaps it didn't refer to those individuals who were visionaries in the truest sense of the word – people who saw beyond what is obvious.

VISIONING

And that is why knowing and believing work where visualizations and affirmations often do not. Visualizations and affirmations are often mouthed and usually, thought about a great deal. But I have found that so often, when people say affirmations or consciously do visualizations, they do both kind of one-dimensionally – lacking any real passion or strong, full-bodied belief, so they are therefore, not pervasive.

I find affirmations are frequently little more than lip-service, especially when they are said out loud. For me, saying an affirmation out loud diffuses the energy and scatters the thought and actually puts what I am affirming in question . . . making me more subtly aware of the fact that I am affirming it just because I do not have it; and I therefore become even more aware of what it is I feel I am lacking. This is very insidious because it all takes place on a very subtle, subliminal level . . . a level which is very powerful.

If I ever were to say affirmations, I would say them either internally over and over, or in a very soft voice (perhaps even crescendoing and decrescendoing), almost like a chant. Then at least, the affirmations would take on some emotion, some energy, some incantatory quality that could be effective – especially in tricking the mind through the hypnotic power of rhythm and suggestion.

But to merely say an affirmation in an ordinary way (which is what most people do) without adding any sense of urgency, or constant repetition or an incantatory quality – I believe has either little or no effect . . . or is often even counterproductive . . . doing more harm than good.

So an affirmation said as a one-dimensional mental exercise often serves to further remind a person of the very thing that he or she feels the lack of and is therefore affirming. In so doing, it often undermines the very belief that the affirmation is trying to affirm.

The same is true of visualizations – if they are not done with an intense, passionate, unwavering belief buttressing them – they become mere reminders of what you *don't* have that you want . . . and actually hinder you in getting what you want.

What I call visioning – which is not a consciously initiated activity – is what I find really works. And the beauty of visioning is that it is not anything you have to do. It just happens.

Once you have a burning desire to be rich (or anything else you want) and decide to do, be or have it, and then act on your decision; once you proceed to act with a strong, passionate, unwavering, full-bodied pervasive belief that you will get it . . . the visioning just appears and grows larger and more real – fleshing out and becoming more substantial – every day and with every act you take.

You begin to live what it is that you desire as what you desire becomes so real, so palpable for you that it is no longer just a thought, a need or a desire. It is something that you find yourself living and breathing every single day. So it takes on a life and momentum of its own and carries you along.

It is almost as though the result or the end you are visioning becomes your starting point. The end becomes the beginning because what you want is so real for you that you are already experiencing it as a reality and your daily life is then, just moving you through the actions and activities that are catching your life up with the reality you are already experiencing, living and already know and feel with certainty is real.

If you have any doubts about this or feel at all confused about how it works, remember Christopher Columbus describing to David, the new world that wasn't even visible to the eye yet! This is what I call *full-bodied visioning . . . being a visionary . . . possibility living . . . living "as if."*

A lot of people say, "Oh, you mean 'Fake it 'til you make it,'" . . . and I say, "No, I don't!" This has nothing to do with faking anything. This has to do with believing something so much – that you see it "in the flesh," "in the world . . . in *your* world" already. This has to do with certainty, with living with such a certainty, that the certainty creates the reality because according to the laws of nature – with that kind of certainty and knowing – the reality *has to* evolve and reveal itself. It has no choice.

It's a conundrum almost like the perennial "chicken and the egg." Which comes first? Does the reality you are visioning, living and feeling already exist in some ideal form, as Plato tells us it does . . . and are you just seeing into that ideal reality before it becomes manifest? Or are your belief and passion so strong that they are creating the reality?

Perhaps the best explanation is that your strong, unwavering belief acts like *the organizing principle* – creating order out of chaos, creating the reality you want and envision out of a myriad of possible realities – like the kaleidoscope creates a unique reality each time you turn it, out of the disparate, unorganized elements and possibilities.

Without getting deeply into quantum physics and philosophy . . . what I am saying is that your thoughts . . . your beliefs . . . when they are infused with passion, constancy and intensity . . . are as powerful as a laser and a magnet. They can create order out of chaos; they can create something where there seemingly was nothing before – and your beliefs can create and bring to you whatever it is you desire. They can make you rich, happy, healthy – anything you want. You just have to believe.

As Claude Bristol, in his wonderful book, *The Magic of Believing* wrote:

> . . . *most of the sustained and continuing manifestations come as a result of belief. It is through this*

belief with its strange power that miracles happen and that peculiar phenomena occur for which there appears to be no known explanation. I refer now to deep-seated belief – a firm and positive conviction that goes through every fibre of your being – when you believe it "heart and soul" as the saying goes. Call it a phase of emotion, a spiritual force, a type of electrical vibration – anything you please, but that's the force that brings outstanding results, sets the law of attraction into operation, and enables thought to correlate with its object. This belief changes the tempo of the mind or thought-frequency, and, like a huge magnet, draws the subconscious forces into play, changing your whole aura and affecting every-thing about you – and often people and objects at grand distances. It brings into your individual sphere of life results that are sometimes startling – often results you never dreamed possible.

So if you really want something – whether it's to be rich, famous, happy, healthy, to meet your soul-mate, write a book . . . whatever it is you want – just decide to be it, have it, do it . . . then do something to achieve it and keep on doing things . . . and as you do, begin to live it . . . allow yourself to live it . . . to believe with every fibre of your being that you *deserve* to do, be and have it; that you *can* do, be and have it . . . and that you *will* do, be and have it.

Expect it and live as though what you expect is on its way to you. You have to believe in miracles; otherwise they won't happen. When you believe in them and expect them – you create the space for them and invite them into your life like a welcomed guest.

Napoleon Hill said, "Faith [belief] is the starting point of all accumulation of riches." Start now to accumulate and claim the riches that are yours.

BELIEVE!

BELIEVE THAT YOU <u>DESERVE</u>
TO BE RICH . . .

BELIEVE THAT YOU <u>CAN</u> BE RICH . . .

BELIEVE THAT YOU <u>WILL</u> BE RICH . . .

<u>EXPECT</u> TO BE RICH . . .

AND THEN JUST <u>LET IT HAPPEN</u>!

ACTION TIPS - STEP 3

*F*irst – let me reiterate that **it is not necessary to do any of these suggestions or exercises.** Just read each chapter in one sitting, with your full attention – no multi-tasking, no interruptions, no distractions. Each chapter is enough to help you accomplish what you want.

Also, when you read the chapters, do not underline or highlight anything as you read. Doing so just interferes with the momentum and stops the smooth, osmotic flow of energy from the chapter through to you. Underlining and highlighting alter the entire process and the connection between you and the material you are reading by putting the receptive, responsive side of you (your right brain) in direct conflict with the "take charge" side (your left brain).

I offer these suggestions, exercises and homework with each step only for those who feel they want to do more.

1. Focus in specifically on what you want and then let yourself embody it and inhabit it completely. What you want should be specific and concrete – not just "I want to be rich" or "I want to be happy." You need to determine and focus in on what you want to do with the money; what will make you happy. Focus in on these and then just begin living and acting as though you already have or are it. Don't complicate the process with visualizations or affirmations. Don't *mentalize* (my own word that I just

invented) it. Just do it . . . Let yourself go – trust, believe, have faith and let the result be your starting point and begin living from there. It works! It really does.

2. Read *The Magic of Believing* by Claude Bristol. It's a fabulous book published in the 1940's that is simple, direct and gets right to the heart of things.

3. Begin noticing the small miracles and "little serendipities" that occur in your life – often every day, but most people never notice them. When you open up and awaken to something, it begins to happen more and more.

*"If the only prayer you said in your life
was "Thank you,"
that would suffice."*

Meister Eckhart

5

STEP FOUR

BE grateful

*G*ratitude is a hugely important step in becoming rich or getting whatever you want in life.

Gratitude is so misunderstood and incompletely understood that it is really necessary – as in the previous three steps – to define it, so that when I use the word, you and I both know that we are referring to the same thing. It is essential that we both agree on what gratitude is before we can determine and discuss how it works to make you rich and help you get what you want in life.

Most people think of gratitude as reactive – a response to something someone does for you or something you receive. But that is too limiting and perhaps why many people don't live with gratitude, but only experience it occasionally.

Gratitude is not reactive. It does not need to wait for someone or something to act upon you to set it in motion. Gratitude is an attitude, a way of living – an active quality in and of itself. It is a natural response to being alive . . . an attitude about yourself and your life that is exhibited in everything you do and say.

Rather than being object-based – contingent upon and reacting to a situation, person or event outside of you – gratitude is deep-rooted and grows organically out of who you are. It is quite simply . . . your response to being alive.

So gratitude is our innate response to our "human beingness," to our being alive and in the world as we move through it and experience it . . . rather than merely being a knee-jerk reaction to people, things or events that we encounter.

ACTIVE GRATITUDE

So many people think of gratitude as merely an emotion. It is not. An emotion is often fleeting and spontaneous. Gratitude is much more elemental than that.

Rather than being an emotion, gratitude is a quality of our character – one of our core values that determines the way we choose to live every single day. And as a quality of our character, it is therefore, totally within our control rather than being a capricious, random reaction to life.

We initiate our own experience of gratitude. So, instead of being passive recipients of events or "so called" gifts that cause us to feel gratitude, we *live* gratitude . . . we act with gratitude.

Perhaps the best way to explain what gratitude is, is to compare it with another element of character – honesty.

You don't say, "That situation or that experience makes me feel honest." Your honesty, authenticity and integrity are a part of who you are – they help define and shape you . . . just like gratitude does.

Honesty, integrity and authenticity – like gratitude – are qualities of your character and they are not therefore, contingent upon external situations, people or events to elicit them from you.

You either are honest, authentic and integrous – or not – in whatever degree you choose to be or are capable of being. But honesty is not an emotion. It is not a feeling with which you react fleetingly to things.

It is instead, how you respond to life, people, events and situations on a regular basis – not merely a knee-jerk, fleeting reaction to external circumstances as they occur.

It is what I call "active gratitude," which is really quite redundant – but seems necessary to counterbalance the misconceptions people have about gratitude.

RESPOND TO LIFE WITH GRATITUDE

So now that we have determined that gratitude is active, not passive . . . that it is a quality of character that can initiate, and responds organically, rather than merely waiting stoically and idly by to be acted upon so it can react – it is obvious that gratitude is imbued with energy.

And because it has energy, it functions according to the laws of nature in which everything is energy.

Perhaps you have heard the phrase, "The energy flows to where the attention goes." Well, just as with the preceding three steps – the energy goes to what you decide, act upon and believe – the energy also goes to what you are grateful for.

You always get more of whatever it is you focus on. So, if you focus on what you are grateful for, you will automatically attract more of that into your life.

If you move through life with gratitude, that responsiveness you have and express to life creates, magnetizes, attracts and elicits – whatever word you want to use – a responsiveness from life back to you.

It really is not nearly as mysterious as it sounds. To take it out of the realm of the abstract . . . just think of your relationships with people. Don't you respond much more happily, readily and better to people who respond to you than those who don't?

Well, it's that simple. It really is. Think of "life" as just another relationship. Your relationship with "life" is a two-way street – you can't just keep asking for and expecting things from life without responding to life. It's like a friendship or a marriage – a partnership – a give and take.

Your spouse or best friend is going to respond much more readily and frequently to you if you appreciate him or her and express sincere gratitude for whatever he or she does for you. That expression of gratitude makes him or her want to do even more for you . . . to give you even more.

I know it may seem weird to you to think of "life" as a spouse, a friend or a relationship, but if you do, I believe that many of the abstract, metaphysical laws and principles of the universe that so many of you may have been studying, reading about and trying to grasp and incorporate into your lives and belief system – will become far more real for you, easier to understand and much more easily incorporated into your behavior and belief system . . . and therefore . . . your life.

THE DANCE OF LIFE

Once you grasp the fact that all of life is really a dance – an exquisite "cosmic" dance between you and life, which you can choreograph however you want – perhaps you will begin to loosen up, enjoy the dance, maybe even become a little creative and start to take risks . . . and most importantly . . . to realize that you are an active participant in and co-creator of the dance, who can make any initiative move you want.

So – getting back to gratitude – if you move through life with gratitude, if you respond to being alive by being grateful, rather than waiting for something you deem "wonderful" to happen to make you feel grateful, then you will find your life expanding more and more, filling up more and more with the things that you are grateful for.

As you experience what you already have with gratitude, what you have will expand and grow into more of what you want. And as you focus on what you want and what you like, what you don't want and don't like will eventually just fall away because you are not putting any attention on it or energy into it.

This happens, often with little or no effort on your part. What you don't want is literally just pushed or crowded out by what you are grateful for and do want. It really is quite magical . . . and serendipitous.

Plus, it feels so good to be grateful. It fills your heart with such joy when you are grateful, that joy spills over into everything and everyone around you – multiplying your joy and things to be grateful for exponentially.

TAPPING INTO THE ABUNDANCE OF THE UNIVERSE

One last note about gratitude. Many people sometimes find it difficult to live gratefully because they live their lives comparatively. This is anathema to success of any kind. To compare yourself, your chances of getting rich, being happy or succeeding . . . or comparing anything of yours to another, is like plucking out the heart and soul of your ability to accomplish these things.

When you are comparing, you are other-directed and always looking outside of yourself. Not only are you looking outside of yourself, but you are depleting your energy resources by looking with an attitude that the "more" of life is out there, and not something to be attained by or from anything organic or from within you.

Living life comparatively is rooted in a belief in a limited universe with limited supply. It's based on a view of the world in which if you cut a piece of the pie and give it to someone else, then there is less for you; that if someone has more than you do, then somehow your chances, opportunities and ability to become as rich, happy, healthy or successful as they are, diminish.

This however, is not the case. The universe is abundant and unlimited . . . and supply is infinite. And because everything is energy – and energy responds to and increases with momentum – the more others have, the more possible it is for you to tap into that same abundance.

Again, to take all of this out of the realm of the metaphysical and abstract and to make it simple, understandable and real for you . . . it's just like being at a party or going to see a comedy at the movie theatre.

Just think of the abundant universe as a party you go to. The more people at the party who are dancing, laughing and having a good time – the easier it is for you to tap into that same energy and have fun and let loose and dance.

The same is true when you go to see a comedy at a movie theatre. Have you ever gone to see a comedy and you were the only one in the theatre? Not much fun, is it? It's hard to get into the hilarity of anything when you are sitting in a big theatre by yourself. But when the theatre is full and everyone is laughing, you can get right into the joviality and enjoy the film much more easily. As a matter of fact, the bigger the room and the more people who are in it, the more contagious the laughter becomes.

That's how the abundant universe works – the more others have, the happier they are, the richer they are – the more happiness and riches there are for you to tap into and share and enjoy. And conversely (or is it inversely? I'm still not sure) the happier and richer you are – the more happiness and riches there are for others to tap into, enjoy and share.

BEING GRATEFUL

So, practice "active gratitude." Let yourself be grateful. Be grateful for the abundant universe you live in. Be grateful that you are alive! Be grateful for, notice and appreciate the blue sky above, the crisp fresh air that tickles your nostrils as you walk along a mountain trail. Be grateful for the small, big and infinite miracles and wonders you experience every day . . . and watch those miracles expand and grow larger and more magnificent with every grateful breath you take.

Be grateful that you can walk. About seven years ago, my mother, who always ran circles around me and my sister and still is a blithe spirit, began to have difficulty walking without a lot of pain and some assistance, as she began using a cane and then, a walker.

Be grateful if you can see. Three years ago, my mother's eyesight began to diminish and now she is considered legally blind.

Don't take anything for granted. Don't overlook the "small" things for the bigger things that "seem" more important or more compelling. They are not.

Be grateful for every act you take that moves you closer to being rich or whatever it is you desire. No matter how small the action may be, no matter that occasionally, it may even seem like the wrong action. Be grateful that you can make mistakes; that you can choose what to do and what not to do; that you can alter and adjust your choices, course and actions like a navigator alters his ship's course to get to where it is going.

As long as you know where you want to go, you will get there. In the meantime, be grateful . . . and enjoy the journey.

A POEM

At the beginning of my book, *Living Serendipitously . . . keeping the wonder alive*, I have excerpted a quote from one of e. e. cummings' poems. I have only quoted four lines, but they are magnificent, life-altering . . . and will fill you with immense gratitude for life.

I recite these lines to myself every morning before I open my eyes . . . every night when I close my eyes just before going to sleep . . . and often, when I am walking through the mountain trails or stop by the waterfall or look up at the sky. These four lines fill me with such joy and peace every time I say them . . . and I know they will you too.

> *i thank You God for most this amazing*
> *day: for the leaping greenly spirits of trees*
> *and a blue true dream of sky; and for everything*
> *which is natural which is infinite which is yes.*

> *e. e. cummings*

ACTION TIPS - STEP 4

1. Today, just notice everything wonderful in your life. Notice all the small, seemingly insignificant things you often take for granted or don't notice. When you go to work today, notice something new that you never paid attention to before. Notice something wonderful about people you pass on the street. When you look in the mirror, notice something beautiful about yourself . . . and smile and be grateful for it.

2. Spontaneously recite a *Gratitude List*. When you wake up and before you open your eyes and start your day . . . and when you get into bed and close your eyes to go to sleep . . . say ten things (or five or seven, whatever number works or has significance for you) you are grateful for. Again, I find it more effective for me if I say them silently. If it works better for you to say them aloud or to write them down, then do that. You know yourself and what works for you better than anyone else does.

3. Start smiling more . . . and you will soon begin to notice that people are smiling back at you more as you walk down the street. People will begin to nod to you, acknowledge you and say "hi" to you . . . even strangers . . . and life will start to acknowledge and respond to you more too.

4. As you do this and make it a habit, you will find that it begins spilling over into every aspect of your life . . . you will find that you have much more energy, you are happier; you will find yourself giving compliments to others much more freely and often, because you are always noticing so much beauty. You will find that your gratitude for the small things, the simple things, brings more and more and bigger and bigger things into your life for you to be grateful for.

"Carpe diem!
Rejoice while you are alive; enjoy the day; live life to the
fullest; make the most of what you have."

Horace, Ancient Roman Poet

STEP FIVE

Rejoice is such a nice word – a word we don't use often enough.

Just the sound of it is happy . . . the cadence lively. When I say the word *rejoice*, it makes me smile and feel good.

And those are things we "modern folks", especially us westerners, often place little value on. We push ourselves so hard, so relentlessly as we seamlessly move from one challenge to the next and the next and the next, without ever taking time to pause . . . to congratulate ourselves on and celebrate our accomplishments.

Even the hardiest thoroughbred needs moments of rest to renew and replenish his strength and stamina and resolve, so he can run the next race at peak performance. He needs rewards and a pat on the back to let him know that he has done a good job, run a good race.

Primitive societies and ancient civilizations understood this and created rituals and ceremonies to honor and acknowledge people's achievements.

We don't do this anymore.

Primitive societies understood the elemental need of all people for recognition and acknowledgement, both of which lead to a sense of completion – a sense of satisfaction – that allows us to move on to our next goal – the next thing we want to do . . . with our full attention, power and focus.

THE IMPORTANCE OF FEELING COMPLETE

I remember reading about this *modern malaise* – the chronic and pervasive feeling of "incompleteness" – that so many people drag along behind them like a burlap sack of cumbersome chalky stones . . . leaving a trail of tiny flakes of residue with each step they take.

Rather than taking the time to celebrate and rejoice in their accomplishments each step of the way, so many people think only of their goal, the end result they are seeking – and fail to . . .

or sometimes just refuse to . . . congratulate themselves on their incremental, but very essential successes along the way.

They rush through everything they do without ever allowing themselves to enjoy, relish and savor each step. They think doing so is a luxury or an indulgence. It's not. It's a necessity.

It is imperative that we allow ourselves to experience the thrill of accomplishment along the way and not wait until the end . . . but rather, as we proceed. That's what helps us proceed and continue moving forward with gusto. That sense of accomplishment we feel when we rejoice in our small successes, fills us with a sense of satisfaction that makes us feel complete and therefore, whole and powerful.

If we do not experience this completion – or closure, as some people call it – we may find ourselves looking for external validation all the time because we have not completed the process . . . not closed the circle. So, as we proceed on to the next, and the next project or step in our road to success, riches and happiness – we are always carrying a remnant or lingering residue of incompleteness and dissatisfaction along with us, which hinders us and often prevents us from becoming rich, successful, happy, or whatever it is we are seeking.

SAVOR YOUR LIFE AND YOUR SUCCESSES

To take it out of the realm of the abstract . . . not taking the time to rejoice in your successes is like eating fast-food or gulping down a meal without really chewing your food or even tasting it, just so you can finish your meal and rush off to do the next thing you want or need to do.

When you do this, you usually wind up eating more than you need because you ate so fast that the food doesn't have time to digest before you realize you are full . . . or you don't eat enough and then are hungry as soon as you get up from the table. Either way, it's not very satisfying.

But when you go out to *dine*, you *do* take the time. You take the time to enjoy your meal . . . to actually *savor* your food, so that when you finish, you feel comfortably satiated and experience a sensation of completion.

Savoring our food is like savoring our life . . . two things we don't do often enough. In our fast-paced society, we rush through just about everything without even allowing ourselves the privilege of really enjoying our experiences . . . without being fully present as we are experiencing them.

Savor is a wonderful word! A word we don't use nearly enough. It's a sensuous word . . . a word that makes whatever we are doing almost palpable. And *savoring* is an activity we don't engage in enough. *Savoring* takes time . . . it requires that we relax . . . that we let go . . . that we are fully present, rather than thinking about what we are going to do next.

Taking the time to savor your small successes, satiates you and fills you with a sense of completion so you can move easily and fluidly and totally onto the next thing, without any excess baggage or feeling of incompletion that needs to be filled or satisfied . . . without any sense of longing or need for recognition left unfulfilled.

Taking the time to rejoice and celebrate your small successes also energizes you, and empowers you to create even more successes . . . and bigger ones.

Celebrating and rejoicing – like gratitude – bring more of what you celebrate and rejoice into your life. They create a momentum and a magnetic field that keep expanding and making your experiences and your life larger and richer. "The more you praise and celebrate your life, the more there is in life to celebrate," says Oprah Winfrey.

LETTING GO

There are even physical benefits to rejoicing, celebrating and savoring your successes on your path to becoming rich or getting anything you want. When you do so, you release your pent-up, type A energy – that *adrenalin energy* that is so necessary for you while you are in active focus mode.

It's like breathing. You can't just keep inhaling. At some point, you also have to exhale . . . so you can take in more air and inhale again. Otherwise, you're just holding your breath . . . and there is only so long you can continue doing that.

When you rejoice and celebrate however, you relax, you let go . . . you exhale. Only by taking the time to congratulate yourself and enjoy your accomplishments can you multiply those resources so you can increase and expand what you accomplish. If you don't take the time to rejoice and celebrate, eventually you will deplete yourself and your resources.

So many people decide, act, believe and are even grateful . . . but still hold their breath . . . waiting . . . waiting anxiously and breathlessly for IT to happen.

But to close the circle, to complete the manifestation and realization of what you want – you need to let go. You need to celebrate and rejoice as if IT has already happened just as you envision and want it to.

You can't hold IT too tight or you will suffocate IT . . . suffocate the dream – the riches you want. You must let the dream breathe because only in that way will it become alive and vital and keep growing and expanding.

So once you have decided to be rich . . . and you act on that decision and keep acting . . . and you believe that you will be rich, believe that you deserve to be rich and believe that you are going to be rich . . . once you begin to express your gratitude for all that you are and all that you have right now at this very moment in your life . . . then . . . allow yourself to luxuriate in the knowing that you have done and are doing everything you need to do in order to become rich, happy, successful, in love – whatever it is you want – and rejoice and celebrate.

Let go your tight grip . . . and set your dream free as you remain unwavering in your decision, actions, belief and gratitude. Give yourself permission to dance, to sing, to laugh, to rejoice in the fruits of your hard . . . or rather . . . your "smart" labor.

To rejoice and celebrate is a declaration of unconditional trust and thanksgiving . . . and few things act more powerfully than these two as a claim upon the unseen forces in the universe to help you get what you want. As the German philosopher and mystic Meister Eckhart said, "If the only prayer you said in your life was 'Thank you,' that would suffice."

RE-CHOICING

The dictionary says the word *rejoice* comes from the French. I am reminded of a wonderful French phrase – *joie de vivre* – which really has no English equivalent. It literally translates into "joy of life."

The definition of *rejoice* is "to feel joy and great delight." When you rejoice, you realign yourself with joy. After your hard work, your focus, your consistent actions and belief – after all these steps that require mobilization of your resources and energy – you let go so you can realign yourself with joy.

You realign yourself with your source that enables you to do and accomplish all things. And in that way, rejoicing reconnects you with who you are – with your divinity. It reconnects your human and your Godlike self.

It is almost as though you are on a string that begins at your core and stretches out, giving you all the latitude and leeway you need to explore, to move, to proceed unwaveringly outward toward whatever it is you want to accomplish . . . allowing you to step into that adrenalin energy, that laser focus, that superhuman empowerment and boldness that are required for you to decide, to act, to believe and to continue . . . When you are grateful and take time to rejoice, you touch your humanness again. You become human, humble and soft again – pliable and flexible – ready and able to be shaped and molded again by all that is true and divine in you . . . all that calls forth and beckons what is best in you.

When you rejoice, you reconnect with yourself, with your source, your core – you reconnect with why you do what you do . . . with why you are alive – for the sheer joy of it all.

When I say the word *rejoice*, I find myself thinking of the word *choice* – or *re-choice*. Partially, I am sure, because they sound so much alike. But also, I wonder if perhaps they are not intimately connected. Perhaps when we rejoice, we are satisfying something elemental and deep inside us . . . and by doing so . . . we liberate ourselves to make better choices based on the completion and satisfaction we experience as a result.

Perhaps when we rejoice and celebrate, we complete a cycle and allow ourselves to move on with our full power and being, to whatever it is we want to do or accomplish next.

Perhaps when we rejoice, we are actually *re-choicing*. *Re-choicing* with our whole heart – with our passion undiluted, our resolve undissipated, and distilled down to its essence. . . so it is pure, focused, authentic and whole.

Perhaps when we rejoice, we are making a declaration that we are ready – ready to succeed . . . ready to be rich . . . ready to love . . . ready for whatever it is we want to do next . . . whatever Life wants to give us.

Success won't come to someone who isn't ready. Love won't come to someone who isn't ready. And riches and money and abundance and prosperity won't come unless you are ready.

So as you proceed on your path to riches . . . remember to rejoice . . . to announce and celebrate your readiness to proceed and receive all the riches you desire . . . and you will.

12 IDEAS ON HOW TO CELEBRATE LIFE
and
HOW TO LIVE LIFE AS A
JUBILANT JOURNEY

1. Live life from a spiritual foundation.

2. Make a conscious decision to enjoy life.

3. Always have a dream.

4. Don't sweat the small stuff (it's all small stuff).

5. Laugh – (laugh hysterically at least once a day).

6. Smile – a lot.

7. Treat others the way you want to be treated.

8. Share your God-given gifts and talents.

9. Work like you don't need the money.

10. Sing like nobody's listening.

11. Dance like nobody's watching.

12. Love like you've never been hurt.

ACTION TIPS – STEP 5

1. To celebrate one of your successes, take a whole day and just relax, rejoice, have fun – do something frivolous – or do nothing . . . stay in your sweats or your PJ's all day . . . and give yourself permission to enjoy it . . . to luxuriate in it . . . to indulge in whatever you do or don't do – totally, whole-heartedly and unconditionally.

2. To acknowledge something you have accomplished, treat yourself to something – an ice cream cone, a movie, a spa treatment, a free day – without thinking of what you "have" to do, of what you "should" be doing. And actually say "thank you" to yourself for this treat . . . this reward. You will be amazed at how complete and satisfied it makes you feel when you not only do something to reward yourself, but also acknowledge that you are rewarding yourself for your accomplishment, thanking yourself for a job well done.

3. The next time a friend, family member, associate or anyone compliments you on something you've done or accomplished, thank them unabashedly, graciously and whole-heartedly, as someone who knows you fully deserve the compliment. Rejoice in the compliment . . . luxuriate in it . . . Let it complete you and satisfy you . . . and allow yourself to feel good about yourself and what you are doing and accomplishing.

"We make a living by what we get,
but we make a life by what we give."

Winston Churchill

7

STEP SIX

∫HƏRE

There's another quote I love, source unknown . . . "'When I grow up, I want to become a philanthropist!' Johnny said. 'Why Johnny,' his mother replied, 'that's wonderful.' 'Yeah,' Johnny responded, 'they all seem to have a lot of money.'" Which shows that Johnny is no dope!

But seriously – I remember when I was growing up – one of my favorite TV shows was *The Millionaire*. In it, a round-faced, dark-haired man named Mr. Tipton – dressed in a suit and tie (black and white of course, since all the TV's were then) always showed up at somebody's front door with the announcement that he was there to give the person a check for one million dollars! He always explained that there were no strings attached to the gift (and I am sure, all taxes were paid . . . although at the time, the thought never even entered my mind).

The recipient of the million dollars was always flabbergasted, totally unsuspecting . . . and always worthy in some ordinary way.

And since for me, the highlight of the show was always that moment when Mr. Tipton knocked on the door and announced that he was giving the person on the other side of the door one million dollars – anonymously and unconditionally, it thrilled me so much, that I don't even remember anything else about the show . . . not even one single episode.

But here's the amazing thing – something I am actually only just realizing right now, this very moment, as I am writing this – the thrill for me . . . what has stayed with me all these years . . . was the desire to be Mr. Tipton and his anonymous benefactor . . . *not* the recipient! Wow!

How amazing that for me – even as a child – the thrill was in the giving, not the getting. Now don't get me wrong – I am not a martyr, not at all saintly . . . and I never even really considered myself very altruistic . . . certainly not nearly as altruistic and selfless as many of my friends are.

In fact, as an artist and a writer – an identity that emerged quite early in me – I was often egotistical and quite self-centered. Even so, I still never lost my fascination with . . . my deep, unwavering desire to be Mr. Tipton and his anonymous benefactor – the one *giving* the money, not the one getting it.

And apparently, my thrill of being and doing so, had nothing to do with how the million dollars changed the people's lives or with receiving recognition as the benefactor. Otherwise, I would remember the rest of the show . . . at least one episode . . . of how someone's life was changed by this gift.

But no – the complete and total thrill for me was that one moment when Mr. Tipton announced why he was standing there at the person's front door. And it was Mr. Tipton and his boss who I always wanted to be – *not* the new millionaire!

Apparently, this act of giving touches some need, some desire in us that is so elemental and pure, that even as a little girl, I responded to it.

I originally began to tell you the story of *The Millionaire* just as an example of . . . a segue into the subject of sharing, giving and philanthropy – but as I wrote this, I realized how powerful a story it really is . . . how powerful the show's impact was on one little girl . . . and how it tells us about what is really important to people on a gut, visceral level.

SAVED BY PHILANTHROPY

I am reminded of the story of George Soros – a great philanthropist. Soros was and is an American global financier, born in Hungary in 1930. Many people questioned how he had made his money and I had read that years ago therefore, he was not readily accepted by the wealthy and "high" society . . . not even perhaps, well liked or respected by them.

About twenty years ago, I remember reading about him . . . that he was going through a difficult and nasty divorce (as I am sure you can imagine with all that money and power up for grabs – the stuff movies are made of).

After the divorce, he found himself terribly depressed. This man, who is one of the richest in the world, said he tried everything to alleviate his depression – he traveled, he philandered, he partied, he bought things, he built houses (or rather, mansions) . . . he did everything he could think of . . . everything money could buy. Nothing helped.

Then – he found philanthropy. And in the article I read, he was quoted as saying, "Philanthropy saved me."

That statement made such a huge impression on me when I read that . . . perhaps it was that little girl again in front of her black and white television set – her dream of being a philanthropist awakened again . . . the joy of it corroborated by this powerful, famous man. (By the way, George Soros is highly respected and well liked today.)

So sharing is not something you do just because you are generous, or because you are nice. Sharing is something you do because you cannot *not* do it. It is compelling . . . It is gratifying . . . It is something you simply *have* to do.

When you become rich and successful, you will find that you are like Nietzsche says he was when he wrote his book

Thus Spake Zarathustra . . . he felt "like the bee that hath gathered too much honey," and that "this is the hardest of all: to close the open hand out of love, and keep modest as a giver."

When you become rich, you become like George Soros . . . "like the bee that hath gathered too much honey," you spill over simply because you cannot not spill over and still exist.

So why wait until you have your million dollars in the bank. Why not begin sharing while you are in transit – on your way to becoming a millionaire?

Since "the idea becomes the reality," and since it is no longer a matter of *if*, but rather *when* you will be rich, once you have decided to be; then begin sharing out of that richness that has not yet completely manifested, but is surely on its way.

Many people, as well as religious and spiritual groups, do this by tithing – giving ten percent of all they earn to whatever place, organization or person is the source of their spiritual sustenance and inspiration. Some people tithe informally – by consistently performing acts of generosity.

Whatever works for you, whatever feels right, is the best way for you to share your riches . . . and to give back. There is no right or wrong – only what feels good. Abraham Lincoln said, "If I do good, I feel good; if I do bad, I feel bad. That's my religion."

If something you do makes you feel good – on a gut, visceral level – then it is right for you. Your body – your gut – never lie.

BASK IN THE GLOW OF LARGESSE

I've lived overseas in several foreign countries and have found that sometimes there is a word in one language that, despite all attempts at translation, just has no equivalent in another in terms of sensibility and nuance. The French word *largesse* is such a word for me.

Largesse is defined as "the joy of largeness; great generosity; generosity of spirit or attitude." It is this last definition that comes closest to capturing what *largesse* is – *a generosity of spirit or attitude*.

It is not merely the act of giving. That is too limited and *largesse* is BIG. It's huge.

It is not just generosity – generosity is a giving of or from oneself to another and therefore, implies a *giver* and a *givee* – two separate people connected by an act.

Even philanthropy is linear in this respect.

But *largesse* suggests no distinction – there is no *giver* and no *givee*. No benefactor and recipient. It's fluid – like a liquid in which you can no longer separate the various elements.

It's like the compound you learned about in high school Chemistry. A compound is a totally new entity that is created by the mixing of different elements (as opposed to a mixture in which the different elements retain their own individual identities and do not merge with each other to form a new entity. Funny . . . the things you remember from your childhood.)

So, *largesse* is like a compound – something new and bigger than it was before. Something that can no longer be broken down into its various components – into *giver* and *givee*. There is just *largesse* – the aura of *largesse* . . . the glow of *largesse* in which *givers* and *givees*; benefactors, philanthropists and recipients all bask in its radiant glow together.

So *largesse* means something so much bigger than you are . . . And sharing – sharing your riches – becomes something you *must* do, something you *want* to do, something you are *compelled* to do . . . and something you *long* to do.

Sharing erupts organically out of the richness of your life, spilling over like hot, brilliant lava.

Sharing opens your heart and makes everything larger than just you, so you are not the center of the universe – not the end all and be all of what you sow and reap.

Instead, sharing expands your horizon, expands your focus, so you will "Dare something worthy," as author Joe Vitale says. Dare something more than just money.

Sharing expands your gratification and in so doing – begins to multiply exponentially all that you do, want to do and are capable of doing. It increases all that you have . . . all that you are . . . and all you enjoy.

And besides . . . sharing feels good, so it must be right!

QUOTES ON SHARING

*"Money is like manure; it's not worth anything
unless it's spread around encouraging young things to grow."*

Thornton Wilder

*"A bit of fragrance always clings to the hand that gives the
rose."*

Chinese Proverb

"No one has ever become poor by giving."

Anne Frank

*"Each morning we must hold out the chalice of our being
to receive, to carry, and to give back."*

Dag Hammerskjold

*"It is every person's obligation to put back into the world
at least the equivalent of what he takes out of it."*

Albert Einstein

ACTION TIPS - STEP 6

*C*onsider doing one of the following as you commit to being rich. Doing one or a combination of these three things is not only personally gratifying, but is an act of trust as well as a declaration to God, the universe and your higher self that you *know* you are rich and are therefore, sharing your riches . . . and that you know even more riches are coming to you.

Either

Decide and commit to tithing ten percent on a regular basis of all that you earn, to the place, organization, person or persons from whom you feel you receive your spiritual sustenance, inspiration and motivation. You can change and replace these whenever the sources of your inspiration and motivation change.

Or

Whenever you receive totally unexpected income or money – money you never expected or saw coming – gift (I don't really like the word tithe) whatever, wherever or whomever you feel was the source of that richness coming into your life.

Or

Gift informally – by performing random acts of monetary generosity and giving back. For example:

For your next oil change, go to the more expensive local mechanic who is always checking things for you and doing you favors and not charging you, rather than going to the discount place which will charge you less, but with which you have no personal connection.

Buy a book from your small local, independent bookseller who originally told you about and introduced you to the book, rather than going to the larger chain at which you have a discount card and receive a better price.

THE DARE . . .

So, I dare you to . . .

Dare to be Happy

Dare to Dream

Dare to Prosper

Dare to feel the rapture of being alive

Dare to be all that you can be

Dare to be Delightfully, Delectably,

Deliciously Rich!

*". . . I believe in Bach's Law which says,
'If anything can go right, it must!'"*

Marcus Bach
The World of Serendipity

8

STEP 7

$\int$ERENDIPITY

*N*ow that you're deliciously rich – how do you become delightfully, delectably . . . serendipitously rich?

What's that secret ingredient – that magical 7th step – the key to unlocking the continuous flow of wealth, riches, happiness and success . . . with effortless ease? . . . Serendipity.

Serendipity means eliminating *the hidden shoulds* . . . oh, not the *shoulds* everyone knows about and is aware of. Those are easy . . . or at least easier to deal with.

SILENCING THE HIDDEN *SHOULDS*

It's the hidden ones that are so insidious and prevent us from being happy, rich, successful . . . or whatever we want. It's those hidden *shoulds* whispering in our ear, telling us we *should* be scared, we *should* be anxious, we *should* worry, we *should* be upset . . . we *should this* . . . we *should that* . . . until we don't even know what we are feeling anymore, because these *shoulds* have gotten us so out of touch with our genuine feelings.

It's almost as though we are actors playing a role the way we think it *should* be played, rather than how we want to play it, how we see it being played, how we feel it needs to be played (which we don't even know anymore because we are so focused on and conditioned to how we think it *should* be played). So, we don't dare deviate from those hidden stage directions that those *hidden shoulds* are giving us . . . we don't even allow ourselves the luxury of getting in touch with what we genuinely feel. But it is these genuine feelings however, that will catapult you into authentic living . . . and the riches you desire.

That is the engine behind serendipity. Serendipity is not an accident . . . it's not an occurrence. It's a force that is released when we liberate ourselves from our hidden *shoulds*. And when we do this, we are *in the moment* . . . and that's really what serendipity is all about . . . why it is so organic and *alive* . . . and why it works – because we are *in the moment* all the time, so we can be responsive, present and *alive* . . . and therefore, in touch with what we are feeling . . . so we can take action.

So how do you go from being deliciously rich to seren-dipitously rich? It's simple . . . but not easy . . . because you need to break . . . or rather . . . change that one habit that is so tenacious, so subtle, so insidious that it stops most people from ever becoming rich . . . or whatever else they want.

THE WILLING SUSPENSION OF DISBELIEF

I remember reading years ago, that when you enter a movie theatre, you must enter it with "a willing suspension of disbelief." You must leave your logical, rational mind outside of the theatre . . . in fact, you must leave your mind completely out of it, so that you enter the world of the story – the world created by the writer, director and actors – totally, whole-heartedly, unconditionally.

So that you don't keep asking "how that" or "why this" . . . you don't say, "Wait a minute, that doesn't make sense," because the rules are different in the world they have created and that you have entered . . . and in that world, everything *does* make sense. You just need to accept it and go with the flow.

It's the same in your life – you are the writer, director, and lead actor – and the world you create has its own rules where the impossible becomes possible . . . the impossible becomes probable . . . and anything . . . no . . . everything is possible.

This is the world of your dreams . . . which is not the same as a fantasy. A fantasy is imaginary; a dream is real. And it's not the same as a hope, a desire or a wish either. None of these has any foundation under them . . . there is little substance to them other than a moderate (even sometimes a strong) emotional one.

But a dream . . . a dream is something that grows out of who you are, what you value . . . your deepest desires. A dream is something that the muses bring to us so we can realize it. Goethe, the 18th century German philosopher says, "Whatever you can do, or dream you can, begin it. Boldness has genius, power and magic in it."

So dreams have passion . . . dreams have power . . . dreams are the starting point of great things. And if you dream of being rich . . . you can be!

THE VOICE OF *SHOULD*

So, what is the one habit you must break – *that voice of should*. You need to shut it out . . . turn it off. It's a voice that is so loud and so pervasive . . . that most people don't even hear anything else . . . at the same time, they don't even realize they are hearing this "*voice of should.*"

This "*voice of should*" is the voice that gnaws away at your confidence, your trust, your faith, patience, and peace of mind . . . it keeps telling you that "you *should* be worried, you *should* be afraid" . . . when all the while, deep down inside, you know you are doing what you need to do, you are moving in the direction you want to, and that everything will be just fine.

But that voice says, "Yeah, but it's not now, so you *should* worry . . . you *should* be afraid."

But if you are willing to trust what you *know*, not what you see; if you are willing to trust your *gut* and not your mind; if you are willing to trust *yourself* and not what others say . . . if you are willing to hold firm to your dream . . . then you *will* be serendipitously rich. If you are willing to live richly . . . to be rich *while* you are becoming rich . . . then you are serendipitously rich.

I am not talking about positive thinking, not talking about visualizations or affirmations. I'm not talking about faking it till you make it. There is nothing fake about being serendipitously rich.

Being serendipitously rich has less to do with your mind and your heart than it does with your gut . . . less to do with what you feel and what you think . . . than with what you know.

So, being serendipitously rich is actually not a step . . . it is rather when everything comes together, coalesces and becomes your life. This can happen while you are doing the 7 steps . . . or after . . . but since the 7 steps are not linear, but rather associative and intertwined, becoming serendipitously rich is woven into the very fabric of each and all of these steps – like a hologram, the whole is contained in the parts.

THE FACTS AND BEING RICH

Being serendipitously rich is that moment when you no longer back-slide into the habit of worrying about money and being afraid just because what you are experiencing at the moment – the facts – does not indicate that you are rich.

What are facts anyway? Most people believe that facts are like laws – or mandates from God. That facts are written in stone and cannot be changed. That facts are what they are . . . immutable and unchanging.

But facts are just a statement of what exists at that very moment. They are temporary and situational . . . they describe a present moment observable reality. But facts can change . . . and reality can change. So, facts are not reality. Facts are not "the truth." *The world is flat* was a fact . . . until it became not a fact. *Matter and energy are different* was a fact . . . until it became not a fact.

BEING RICH *BEFORE* YOU ARE RICH

So, to be serendipitously rich, you have to be willing to be rich *before* you are actually rich . . . you have to be willing to see, experience, and live what you *know* to be true, despite what the facts tell you *seems* to be true.

You have to be willing to be who and what you know you are even though others may not be able to see it yet . . . even though you may not be able to tangibly prove it yet. You have to dare to believe . . . dare to allow yourself to know what you know – despite all outward appearances – and to act on what you know . . . and to live it.

You have to be willing to give yourself *permission* to be rich even though you do not yet have the money to prove that you are . . . even though you may feel like you are being crazy, or hypocritical or lying or in denial . . . or maybe just plain delusional . . . but somewhere, deep down inside of you . . . *because you have made the decision to be rich* (or happy or safe or successful or . . . whatever), you *know* that your being rich is no longer a matter of *if* . . . only *when*. And then it becomes a question only of, "Do I dare live like I am rich even though I don't have the money yet?"

And then suddenly, one day, there is no more back-sliding . . . not even the thought of it, because it is now so inconceivable to you, so alien, that you can't even imagine worrying about money or being scared or doubting . . . because being rich is now your life and the fact that you don't have the money yet doesn't even seem to matter. It becomes totally immaterial because you *know* (not just think or believe) that it is on its way . . . you *know* you are rich . . . and you begin to savor and enjoy being *delightfully, delectably, deliciously . . . serendipitously rich* – whole-heartedly, totally and unconditionally.

SERENDIPITOUSLY RICH . . .
THE IMAGE BECOMES THE REALITY

. . . Then one day, quite unceremoniously, the money comes. It gets deposited into your bank account . . . and your account grows and grows . . . and serendipitously rich becomes factually rich while you have been too busy living your serendipitously rich life to even think about money, worry about money, be anxious about money or plan for money . . . you have been too busy living a serendipitously rich life to even notice that suddenly, serendipitously rich and factually rich have become one and the same . . . that the invisible facts – the riches you have known, felt and claimed all along *once you decided to be rich* – are now visible for everyone to see.

And then, it no longer matters if everyone can see the money now because being serendipitously rich has enriched your life so, that the money – once all important while it was lacking – is suddenly only one small part of your wealth now that it is abundant and flowing . . . now that you are doing what you love . . . now that you are in control of your life and your finances . . . because now you know what you need to do, what you *can* do to get *anything* you want . . . even to get rich.

And being serendipitously rich creates a new reality – or rather, new facts – for everyone to see . . . so the facts change . . . and just like "the world is flat" and just like "matter and energy are two different things" were replaced by new facts . . . the facts of your life are replaced by new facts as you step into and claim this new reality . . . this reality that says, that proves, that shows everyone that . . . *YES* . . . *I am rich – I am factually, delightfully, delectably, deliciously . . . serendipitously rich for all to see!*

QUALITIES OF SERENDIPITY

In the Moment

Responsive

Your True Feelings

Facts are not what they seem . . . They can change

Permission

No Shoulds

Letting go

Reality is what you experience, not what you see

Openness

Wonder

Delight

Your Authentic Self

*Allows you to experience reality **before** it becomes
a physical reality*

SHOULDS TO DELIGHT IN . . .

The *voice of should* is very powerful – so use it to your advantage and benefit.

*Here is a new list of **shoulds** for you to delight in . . . enjoy . . . savor . . . live by . . . and . . . even . . . to get rich by!*

Feel free to add to the list . . . and remember to always phrase your new *shoulds* in the affirmative according to what you *do want*, not what you don't. (The Universe, God, your Higher Self, the Organizing Principle does not recognize or respond to the words "no" or "not" . . . and . . . neither do you! People respond to the word [noun, verb, adjective, adverb], not the qualifier that comes before it.)

I *should* be happy.

I *should* be delighted.

I *should* be full of joy.

I *should* be loved.

I *should* have life easy.

I *should* be successful.

I *should* be healthy.

I *should* have money . . . lots of it.

I *should* be rich.

I *should* have what I want.

I *should* be full of energy.

I *should* feel empowered.

I *should* feel vibrantly alive.

I *should* do what I love and love what I do.

I *should* love my life.

I *should* be DELIGHTFULLY, DELECTABLY, DELICIOUSLY RICH · · ·

I *should* be SERENDIPITOUSLY RICH!

ACTION TIPS - STEP 7

1. Begin eliminating those *hidden shoulds* that determine your experiences and shape your life. Begin with one – the one you think might be the easiest to eliminate.

For example . . . the next time someone does or says something that could be hurtful to you, and the voice that tells you "I *should* be insulted" rears its head, stop and ask yourself if you really *are*. Really get in touch with your feelings and wade through the layers of social conditioning telling you what you should and should not feel.

Let yourself move through the whole process of . . . "He/ She shouldn't have said that" . . . "He/She ignored my needs" . . . "He/she was really rude and insulting" . . . "I *should* be insulted."

Then ask yourself, "Am I? What am I *really* feeling?" Most of the time, you will discover that you aren't really insulted at all . . . and that the whole thing really isn't that important . . . that you can easily shrug it off with "Oh, well," . . . or "So what," once you move through and beyond what you think you *should* feel!"

See and feel how liberating that is. Then, once you eliminate one *hidden should* . . . move on to another . . .

Don't take things personally

then another . . . and another, moving on to the more difficult ones that have to do with money (ie: I *should* worry about money, I *should* have to struggle to make money . . . you get the picture . . .) and then eliminating them one by one, so you can become *serendipitously rich!*

The first time you do this exercise, you will actually find yourself feeling shocked and astonished that you really don't care as much as you thought . . . that you are *not really* insulted, you are *not really* worried about money . . . even perhaps, not insulted (or worried) at all. It's an amazing exercise . . . and extraordinarily liberating!!

2. Give yourself permission to be rich (or happy, or successful, or healthy . . . or anything else you want).

It seems that deep down, we are all still (and always will be) little kids needing and wanting permission – permission to be happy . . . permission to have life easy . . . permission to be loved . . . permission to do what we want . . . permission to be rich . . . permission not to struggle.

I know it sounds crazy, but it's true. It seems most people – rich or poor, young or old, professional or blue collar, male or female, successful or struggling . . . operate under a hidden cloud of what Shirley MacLaine calls "underservability."

We struggle to get what we want (because we believe we are *supposed* to struggle) – and then when we get it – we don't feel we deserve it, can't accept it, don't trust it . . . so we sabotage it. Then we continue to struggle even when we don't need to because that's what we think we are supposed to do . . . what we *should* do. (Again, there's that insidious "*voice of should*"!)

So give yourself unadulterated (interesting word!!!), unconditional, absolute permission to be rich! One way you can do this is to elicit it from one of your friends, mentors, spiritual guides, or what I call "your council of advisors." These are the people you love and trust (they can be living or not) who have only your good at heart.

You don't even need to have them all in one place. You can phone them, visit them, meet with them . . . or . . . You can call them together anytime you want in your mind, while walking, out in nature, in your favorite place, meditating, whatever . . . I actually find it much more effective to get permission from each one individually . . . usually the permission that means the most from that particular individual . . . although sometimes I do call the whole council together.

3. Read my book *Living Serendipitously . . . keeping the wonder alive.*

I can't tell you how many people – all kinds, ages, genders, professions and jobs – have told me how liberating and empowering this book was for them . . . because it gave them permission.

Why am I recommending my own book? I always recommend the book I think is the best for whatever I am speaking about . . . and in this case, I believe this is the best book. So, why not recommend it? I recommend others' books when I think they're the best.

4. Do the "Dance of Should" – a crazy, impromptu, totally off-the-wall dance or movements . . . whatever comes to you and whatever you truly feel like doing in the moment . . . with no censorship, no critic, no judge.

Remember (how could you forget?) the memorable dance Elaine did on *Seinfeld*? Or the dance Kevin James did in the film *Hitch*, when he was trying desperately to woo the rich heiress whom he loved, but was unable to contain the secretly mischievous, out of control little kid inside him on the dance floor?

Doing something like that is liberating, fun, and physically expresses your total disregard for those *hidden shoulds* that are trying to dictate the movements of your life.

Doing something like that gets you totally out of your rational, logical mind that sees and accepts only what is appropriate or reasonable . . . and opens you up to the infinite possibilities of wider horizons.

5. Remember the exercise we did at the beginning of the book – throwing the water out of your front door? Well, do it again . . . only this time . . . with every heave of the bucket, declare (silently or out loud, whichever works best for you) that you are hurling out another *hidden should* that has been holding you back from being serendipitously rich!

6. Begin to live what you are dreaming of. Don't think about it, question it, wonder if it's possible, be afraid you look foolish . . . just do it!

Whatever your dream is – *feel it here, now, real* . . . and begin to live and act just like you would if it were real . . . because it *is* real . . . and if you do this . . . soon it will be tangibly real.

Create the immediacy that makes the experience palpable . . . step into it with your whole heart . . . and live it . . . do it now.

*"The riches you receive will be in exact proportion to
the definiteness of your vision, the fixity of your purpose,
the steadiness of your faith and the depth of your gratitude."*

Wallace D. Wattles
The Science of Getting Rich

9

DARE TO BE RICH

*B*eing rich is easy; not being rich is hard. This book is the rich person's guide to easy success.

Yes – I know that sounds like an oxymoron. You don't usually hear those two words together – "easy success" – but that is only because of years, decades and probably centuries of social conditioning that has been passed down, almost by rote, without question.

But success *is* easy – it is we who make it difficult. Success *is* simple – it is we who complicate it. Success *is* fun – it is we who make it drudgery.

So, if success is so easy, why aren't more of us rich and happy and successful? Because we put up roadblocks, detour signs, big stop signs; we build walls and carve out gorges and imagine mountains; we become hard, inflexible, scared; we shrink and become small and timid and try to make ourselves invisible while all the while there is this greatness, this largeness inside us clamoring to get out – the thunderous voice of God reverberating inside us with a magnificence, a mystery, a beauty that we know and feel on some level, but our conscious mind just refuses to believe, accept and allow.

We think we are intimidated by life, by others, by circumstances; but we are not. It is we who intimidate ourselves because on some level we all know and feel our greatness, yet we shrink from stepping into it.

We devise all kinds of methods to avoid ourselves, our greatness and stepping into and claiming the riches, success and abundance that are ours – like procrastination, a whole host of socially and personally acceptable subterfuges, and the entire gamut of defense mechanisms that enable us to still feel OK while avoiding our success and prosperity.

But OK is not good enough . . . and is certainly not acceptable on a long-term basis. In fact, feeling just OK is worse than feeling really bad on a long-term basis. At least when you feel really bad, you know something is wrong and know you need to take some action.

Feeling OK however, lulls you into a false sense of security and comfort . . . a complacency that dulls your mind, your senses, your perceptions and abilities. Feeling OK siphons off your motivation, your passion, your zest for life, your curiosity, your sense of wonder, your desire to achieve, accomplish and aspire . . . slowly draining your energy and depleting your resources – very subtly . . . and therefore, insidiously.

TAPPING INTO ABUNDANCE

Perhaps one of the reasons more people aren't rich and don't live abundantly is because they think abundance is something they have to create. Abundance is not something you create; it is something you tap into. And therefore, money is really something that is somehow "out there," just waiting for you to claim it.

Claude Bristol, in his book *The Magic of Believing*, tells the story of a friend of his who in the 1940's was building a boat, but needed an electric drill to complete it. He didn't want to buy one because he only needed it for a few months for this one particular project, and he couldn't rent it because then he had to return it every morning.

"Then he told me, [Bristol relates] 'I got thinking one night that somewhere there was a drill for me and I would have it placed in my hands.' The more I thought about it, the more I thought it possible."

Well – a few days later, he did get his drill. A friend found out he needed one and loaned it to him.

The key here however, is that Bristol's friend realized that there was a drill for him "out there" and somehow it would find its way into his hands . . . and it did.

The same thing has happened to me over and over with money, things, people, etc. Last year, my son was visiting me in North Carolina and we were playing Horseshoes at the Inn nearby, but were missing one horseshoe. We looked and looked all over, but couldn't find the missing horseshoe.

So we played without it, sharing one of the horseshoes. And then – the strangest thing happened. I *knew* the missing horseshoe was there! I *felt* it. I can't explain how or why. So I stopped all activity, got quiet for a moment – and then walked right over to where the missing horseshoe was and lifted it up out of the bushes.

I have often had experiences like that, but this was different. This time I actually felt its presence – I *felt* the density or the vibration of the horseshoe . . . I *felt* its presence.

And perhaps, that's how it works with money too. Perhaps we just need to accept the fact that the money – the million dollars, the riches (or whatever else you want – your soul-mate, the perfect job, ideal house, etc.) are "out there" just waiting to be placed in your hands, in your life, in your bank account . . . waiting for you to find and claim them.

And perhaps, all we need to do is to get quiet and still – so we can feel the vibratory presence of the money, the person, the home we want and we will be led to it easily, naturally and effortlessly.

That actually happened to me when I was with my son again – in Freeport on Grand Bahama Island. We were in the casino – he was playing the tables and I was playing the quarter slot machines.

Intuition
angels

All of a sudden, I was literally directed – by some voice or "vibratory shift" perhaps – to leave the machine I was playing and go to a large, flashy, modern, automated dollar machine – a machine I never would have chosen to play.

As soon as I began playing that machine, I knew the winnings were there waiting for me to claim them. Every time I put my dollars in, I knew, I could feel some density, some vibration that told me . . . yes, it was getting closer and closer.

After playing the machine eight or ten times (I don't remember which) I won $1,000.00 . . . and I wasn't the slightest bit surprised because I felt the money before it even got into my hands – I knew it was on its way to me – it was there waiting for me to claim it.

If I had not listened to the still small voice urging me to not only switch machines, but directing me to that specific machine . . . If I had not been responsive and decisive and not acted immediately as the voice was urging me to – *do it, do it now, now . . . now* – and if I had not believed unwaveringly in the outcome – everything would have been different.

So, each one of us is a co-creator in the affluence we experience, the "riches" we enjoy with our attentiveness, our responsiveness, our decisiveness, our visioning and our belief.

BEGINNING WHERE YOU ARE

Being, becoming, getting rich . . . acquiring wealth and being affluent all begin with how you are in the world. If you move through life with generosity and graciousness . . . with *largesse – a generosity of spirit or attitude* – then the leap to your finances is not so great; you are already tapped into abundance and just have to expand it to the world of your finances.

And I don't want it to sound overly metaphysical either. It's actually very practical, simple and ordinary – if you want to be rich, you cannot compartmentalize your life, your self and your spirit. You cannot live linearly and anally, with a tight hold on your compliments, your graciousness, your generosity of spirit and then hope, pray, wish or expect that your finances will be overflowing and abundant. You need to overflow in all of life.

I remember taking a course in Hemingway in graduate school . . . and learning that all of his heroes had a dual persona – a business self and a personal self. I thought that sounded absurd at the time . . . so artificial; until years later when I realized that many people actually do live their lives that way. Perhaps they are manipulative at work and then expect to be able to turn it off and be affectionate, compassionate and empathetic at home. Or perhaps they are goal-oriented and driven at work and then expect to be able to be associative and *relate-able* (that is definitely not a word!) at home.

Balance

Often, they are tight and ungiving or ungracious in their relationships and daily living and then expect the riches to flow to them. It doesn't work that way. What we do . . . who we are every day . . . is what we will experience in our lives. If you want an unimpeded flow of money (friends, love, joy, etc.) you have to enter the flow . . . you have to participate in the unimpeded flow . . . you have to become a part of it.

You have to be willing to *live* richly to be, become and get rich. Money is not attracted to those who don't . . . and money finds those who do, an irresistible magnet. If you practice the very simple steps in this book, you will become a magnet for all the riches you desire . . . and you will do it simply, easily, naturally and have fun doing it.

ENJOY . . . PROSPER . . .
AND DARE TO BE
SERENDIPITOUSLY RICH!

THE 7 RIDICULOUSLY EASY
STEPS TO GETTING RICH

- **DECIDE** – *Intend, Commit, Make a Declaration*

- **ACT** – *Be an Active Dreamer, Ignite Your Passion, Just Do it, No Details*

- **BELIEVE** – *Trust, Go by Your Gut Feelings, Expect to Get What You Want*

- **BE GRATEFUL** – *Practice Active Gratitude*

- **REJOICE** – *Celebrate, Relax, Luxuriate in and Savor Your Successes and Life*

- **SHARE** – *Give Back*

- **SERENDIPITY** – *Eliminate the Hidden Shoulds, Dare to Be Rich **Before** You Are Rich*

ACTION TIPS FOR GETTING RICH

DECIDE – Commit. Your subconscious, the universe, God, The Force – the Universal Spirit is not going to commit if you're not. Also, you need to decide so your subconscious knows what you want . . . almost as if you are letting it know what the assignment is. Like in *Mission Impossible* (the old TV series) – they were instructed to read their mission, commit it to memory and then destroy it . . . so it was indelibly imprinted on their psyche, physiology . . . their entire being.

ACT – Create momentum. Stir up the energy. Create a positive force of inertia. Give direction, movement, energy.

BELIEVE – Anchors and fuels. Gives your dream both roots and wings. Lets you soar at the same time it lays a foundation.

BE GRATEFUL – Keeps things running smoothly, without getting clogged up. Attracts to you more of what you are grateful for.

REJOICE – Acknowledges and celebrates your efforts and accomplishments and gives you a sense of completion.

SHARE – Rejuvenates and replenishes you and enlarges your world, scope and horizon. Makes you want to do, accomplish and give even more.

SERENDIPITY – Keeps you *in the moment*, so you can be responsive, present and *alive* . . . and therefore, in touch with what you are feeling . . . so you can take action . . . so you can be rich *before* you are actually rich.

Any time you find yourself asking "Why Me?"
change that to "Why not me?"
It's got to be someone, so why not you?

Serendipity . . . is a faculty in you that expects, experiences and attracts the best.

Serendipity . . . is a faculty in you that enables you to experience the reality of a thing **before** it is even in the physical world . . . so your full-bodied ex-perience helps materialize it.

Serendipity . . . enables you to begin with the result – that which you desire.

Serendipity . . . makes your dream – your deepest desire – what you decide to do, be or have . . . *a fait accompli!*

The Double Dare . . .

So, I double dare you to . . .

Dare to be Carefree

Dare to be Free-Spirited

Dare to Trust What You Know

Dare to be Rich <u>Before</u> You Are Rich

Dare to be Delightfully, Delectably,

Deliciously Rich . . .

Dare to be Serendipitously Rich!

ABOUT THE AUTHOR

*M*adeleine Kay is the Bestselling Author of *Living Serendipitously . . . keeping the wonder alive.* Adventurist, unconventional success and motivation coach . . . and maverick entrepreneur, she has been featured in *Who's Who of American Women* and *Who's Who in the World.*

She speaks four languages, has been a resident of three continents, been a university instructor and international fashion model on two continents, ran her own advertising and marketing agency, wrote commentaries for the CBS affiliate in Miami and was even an actor in film, television and a music video.

Considered America's leading expert on *serendipity*, she brings the wisdom, passion and playfulness of serendipity sprinkled with her own unique brand of practical, down-to-earth common sense to the world of money and personal finances to help people get, claim and enjoy the riches they desire.

She divides her time between Florida, North Carolina and some favorite places in Europe.

BOOKS BY MADELEINE KAY

Living Serendipitously . . . keeping the wonder alive

A lively and joyful read, *Living Serendipitously,* gets you to be an *active dreamer*, living your dreams, not just thinking about them. It captures the joyful essence of "the art of living" and shows you how to feel deliciously *alive*, vibrant and happy every day of your life . . . no matter what your circumstances. Einstein said, "There are only two ways to live your life – as though nothing is a miracle or as though everything is a miracle." *Living Serendipitously* aligns us with the *everything*. (visit www.LivingSerendipitously.com or your favorite bookstore or online store.)

Living with Outrageous Joy

Joy is contagious . . . joy is revitalizing . . . joy is what every one of us wants to feel more of in our lives. This charming little gift book will re-ignite that feeling of joy in your life and your passion for living. Playfully inspiring and motivating, *Living with Outrageous Joy* will delight and revitalize you. It will open you up to the joy and adventure of living your life to the fullest every single day . . . unleashing in you that feeling of *aliveness* that so many of us are longing to feel. (visit www.LivingWithOutrageousJoy.com or your favorite bookstore or online store.)

The UMM Factor . . . (what you need in order to succeed) (e-book)

This groundbreaking book about passion, purpose and prosperity reveals the three things everyone must have in order to succeed. Without all three, it is possible to succeed, but not likely. With them – your success is guaranteed. What are these three magical things? Madeleine Kay calls them *The UMM Factor*. (visit www.UmmFactor.com)

SERENDiPiTOUSLY RICH

How to Get Delightfully, Delectably, Deliciously Rich (or anything else you want) in 7 Ridiculously Easy Steps

For a complete list of *Serendipitously Rich* offerings
and to receive lively and fun bonuses, go to
www.SerendipitouslyRich.com

DELIGHTFULLY, DELECTABLY, DELICIOUS NOTES

DELIGHTFULLY, DELECTABLY, DELICIOUS NOTES

LaVergne, TN USA
28 June 2010
187730LV00002B/213/P